THE DAVID HUME INS

BEYOND THE WELFARE STATE

THE DAVID HUME INSITUTE

Beyond the Welfare State
An Examination of Basic Incomes in a Market Economy

Samuel Brittan and Steven Webb

ABERDEEN UNIVERSITY PRESS
Member of Maxwell Macmillan Pergamon Publishing Corporation

First published 1990
Aberdeen University Press
© The David Hume Institute 1990

British Library Cataloguing in Publication Data

Brittan, Samuel *1933–*
   Beyond the welfare state: an examination of basic incomes in a market economy.
   1. Great Britain. Personal income. Distribution
   I. Title   II. Webb, Steven   III. David Hume Institute
   339.20941

ISBN 0-08-040915-6

Typeset by Hewer Text Composition Services, Edinburgh
Printed in Great Britain by
BPCC-AUP ABERDEEN LTD.

Foreword

The case for the provision of a minimum income for every person or household was first put forward in 1943 as an alternative to the Beveridge Plan by Lady Rhys-Williams. It was embraced by James Meade in his famous post-war attack on collectivist planning, *Planning and the Price Mechanism* (1948). He regarded income support as an integral part of his 'Liberal-Socialist' solution to the problem of reconciling distributional ideals with market efficiency—a theme to which he recently returned in his *Agathotopia: The Economics of Partnership* which this Institute was very pleased to publish last year. My first book, *The Economics of National Insurance* (1952) contains a sympathetic discussion of the idea and, together with Frank Paish, I helped to devise a scheme for the Liberal Party which was considered by the Royal Commission on the Taxation of Profits and Income (1955). The Statistical Director of the Inland Revenue of those days was markedly unsympathetic towards the scheme and it is ironic that he later prepared *Proposals for a Tax Credit Scheme* (Command Paper 5116 1973) which sparked off the next phase of the discussion—his name, Lord Cockfield! Both authors of this Paper have been prominent in the reconsideration of minimum income guarantees and their combined analytical and computational skills have produced this remarkable essay.

It is interesting to note how the objectives of minimum income guarantees have changed through the years. In the late 1940s and early 1950s, it was certainly true that the basic aim rested on the 'social justice' argument. The additional aims very much reflected the circumstances of the time when the idea of the Welfare State contained a strong paternalistic element, as found in the offer of family support in the form of food subsidies and rent restriction. Frank Paish and I wished to combine income support with the abolition of food subsidies and rent restriction, giving the family unit much more control over the allocation of its purchasing power—a thoroughly liberal idea! James Meade supported these proposals but added the additional point that the combining of the income tax with minimum income proposals would offer 'the perfect instrument for the most effective and prompt control over national expenditure in the interest of avoiding inflation and deflation'—a thoroughly Keynesian position!

The earlier schemes and the one advocated in this Paper have much in common, particularly in the joint desire to reduce the number of persons living below some conventional minimum and to remove the unemployment

v

and poverty traps. Both authors of this Paper offer highly original features of their own. Samuel Brittan regards his Basic Income Guarantee not as a handout but as a property right—the poor person's equivalent to the imputed rent from home ownership and unearned income of the rich. If that means accepting that persons will prefer to opt out on a subsistence income rather than aspire to becoming better off, so be it. That would be their right. His argument is cogent and persuasive. Steven Webb performs the mammoth task of turning their proposals into statistical reality. Anyone who has tried to mount an exercise of this kind will know the traps in the path of the unwary. The fiscal implications of integrating family credit, income support and income tax in a sensible way are fully and honestly displayed. The scheme, like its predecessors, comes up against the problem of affordability but the challenge of how to cope with this problem is taken up in valiant fashion by the authors.

As our readers know and expect, the Institute does not hold a collective view on any issues raised by its authors. This necessary disclaimer does not prevent the Institute from commending this Paper as a most valuable contribution to one of the most important contemporary debates about the condition of our society.

Alan Peacock
Executive Director
David Hume Institute
August 1990

Contents

Preface

The verdict on state controlled economies has been given by current events in Eastern Europe and China, where millions of people have sought to change their regimes as soon as political repression has begun to slacken or to vote with their feet by emigrating to the West. But late twentieth century capitalism has its own faults. Rather than split the difference between the two systems, we have investigated in this Paper the more radical option of seeking to combine an unconditional basic income for all with the advantages of prices, markets and decentralised decsions. We have not tried to design a detailed blueprint, but merely to carry the discussion forward.

The early chapters of this booklet present a case for Basic Incomes as a contribution to political economy at the turn of the century. Later chapters go into more detail on the basic ideas and present a feasibility study of the costs and benefits of specific proposals. Each author is responsible for his own chapters and is not committed to the views expressed by the other author. A little overlapping has been unavoidable to allow both authors to develop their arguments. But they have discussed the contents of all the chapters extensively with each other; and all are different as a result of their collaboration.

At least two important studies, James Meade's *Agathotopia* and Hermione Parker's, *Instead of the Dole* appeared when our own investigations were well advanced. They are mentioned extensively in the following pages but it has not been possible to revise everything in the light of their works; and we thought it best to publish our own observations in the form they have now reached as a contribution to the continuing debate. Both authors have had to fit their work on Basic Incomes into a busy schedule, largely concerned with other matters; and the paper is presented as an essay rather than a treatise. Yet even this constraint has its advantages. For Basic Incomes need to advance beyond their present state of intense preoccupation to a minority and enter into the main current of political and economic discussion.

We would like to thank Andrew Dilnot and Michael Prowse for commenting on an earlier draft and the Institute for Fiscal Studies for the use of its facilities, including its tax and benefit model.

Samuel Brittan
Steven Webb
June, 1990

1 The Case for Basic Incomes

Samuel Brittan

The Basic Idea

A Basic Income is a payment received by every person or household adequate to provide a minimum income, based only on age and family status, but otherwise unconditional. There are many advantages. There would be for the first time a floor for everyone, not dependent on complicated contribution records or intrusive scrutiny of personal means. The present disincentives to accepting low-paid jobs arising from the withdrawal of conditional benefits, as income rises, would go. The risks involved in accepting jobs with fluctuating, or profit-related, pay would be reduced.

Most existing social security benefits are contingent. That is they are related to misfortune or conditions such as age, sickness or unemployment. A Basic Income depends, on the other hand, only on very general characteristics such as number of dependents. There are no questions or conditions relating to effort to find work, state of health, contribution records or capital holdings. Basic Incomes would, eventually, replace many existing specific social security benefits. There would always be people with special needs requiring extra sums on a conditional or discretionary basis, but fewer cases than at present.

Most advocates believe that Basic Income payments should take the form of a tax credit to be set off against tax, but received as a positive payment from the state by those with insufficient tax liabilities. Basic Incomes are sometimes called Minimum Income Guarantees and sometimes Social Dividends. There are many other names too, and there are close links with Negative (or Reverse) Income Tax schemes, discussed below.

Beyond these key points, Basic Income advocates disagree about many key features. They also advocate Basic Incomes for many different reasons; and these differences affect the transitional path they would follow and the second best policies they would accept until a fully fledged Basic Income is affordable. The justification given here is from a frankly pro-market and pro-capitalist angle, although it will not be regarded as coming from 'one of us'.

1

The Leaky Net and the Shaky Ladder

Capitalism operates under rules and conventions and is everywhere supplemented by tax and transfer systems. There will always be disagreement on the size and shape of these taxes and transfers. For people will always disagree on the just distribution of income and wealth, and indeed whether there is such a thing. These differences need not be as wide as they are sometimes made to appear and my own attempt to narrow them, drawing on writers from several disciplines, can be found in Appendix 2.

Despite all detailed disagreements, Winston Churchill's idea of a safety net below which no one should fall, and a ladder on which all can rise, has long commanded wide support. Why then not just accept the Welfare State as it has developed over the twentieth century? Is it not intended to provide precisely the safety net emphasised by Churchill?

Unfortunately, despite the transfer of large sums of money—social security is expected to cost £56 billion in 1990–91, and is by far the biggest single category of public expenditure—poverty has not been eradicated, even judged by the modest Government-endorsed minimum provided by Income Support. (The latter is the present day descendant of National Assistance and Supplementary Benefit and derives ultimately from the old Poor Law.)

Thus the first most traditional and widely supported argument for Basic Incomes is *to plug the gaps and loopholes in social security and to reduce the number of people living below the conventional minimum.* More is said about these objectives in later chapters.

The second argument is that, not only the safety net, but the ladder of opportunity itself, is in a shaky condition. This is because *the high rates of benefit withdrawal when the unemployed obtain work, or people with low incomes move up the earnings ladder, produce serious disincentives known as the unemployment and poverty traps.* By these traps I do not mean that take-home pay is literally lower if work is taken or earnings increased. It is bad enough that total deductions on those at the bottom of the ladder are in the 70, 80 and 90 per cent range, rates rightly regarded as excessive and confiscatory when they are levied on the marginal earnings of the better off. Yet marginal withdrawal rates of over 70 per cent were paid by well over 400,000 families in 1989, even according to official figures.[1]

Non-Work Income

But there is a third and more controversial reason for moving from contingent benefit to Basic Income about which it is best to be frank. This is that *it is positively desirable that people should have a means of subsistence independent of needs.* I first espoused the idea in the early 1970s, when looking for ways of separating the libertarian, free choice aspects of capitalism from the puritan work ethic.

The attraction of a fully fledged Basic Income Guarantee to me was—and is—that it would enable people who are content to live at a conventional subsistence scale to do so. For a rich society can afford to have some people 'opting out'. Any work done to supplement this minimum would attract tax, initially at a specially high withdrawal rate, but eventually at no more than the basic tax and national insurance rate.

The hippy, drop-out, work-shy, or merely low-productivity citizen would in effect be told: 'The community is now rich enough to give you two choices: You can "opt out" if you wish and you will receive an allowance which will be far from princely and well below the normal wage; but it will allow you to live, and will also rise as the nation becomes richer; or you can work and go after larger material prizes. Or you can choose your own compromise between the two.' The whole argument about scroungers, and shirkers is eliminated by giving up the attempt to hunt them down.[2]

I realise that this prospect will seem deeply shocking to a number of people who will describe it as a scrounger's paradise. Even some of those who are not morally shocked have been influenced by Charles Murray's argument that even the present conditional benefits encourage a dependency culture.

There are almost certainly some effects along these lines. But I would ask opponents of Basic Income if they are also opposed to investment income, or to personal inheritance, both of which can have very similar effects in the higher economic ranges.

The clue to legitimising some Basic Income Guarantee is to see it not as a handout, but as a property right. What is or is not a property right depends on custom, attitudes and psychology, as well as law. The important characteristics are that such rights should be widely accepted and should change only slowly in content. In other words they should be secure from rapid redefinition or abrogation with each swing of the electoral pendulum.

It is therefore unfortunate that the subject is usually treated purely as an aspect of social security reform—a tradition from which this Paper has not been fully able to escape. It would be just as valid to see the Basic Income aspect as an inalienable part of the return on the national capital.

The former Chancellor, Nigel Lawson, has spoken of a 'nation of inheritors'. Indeed inheritance is likely to play a much greater role than superficial talk of the enterprise culture suggests. But it will still be only a minority that will inherit substantial sums. Even counting imputed rent from home ownership, most people are unlikely to inherit an unearned income remotely near the subsistence minimum. Basic Income would be the equivalent of an inherited, modest competence available in the middle and lower, as well as upper, reaches of the income scale.

Such an income should help with the problem of the underclass—although there are clearly many other factors behind the rise in the number of homeless and beggars on our streets not easily amenable to financial policy. But it would also be helpful among other groups: artists at the beginning of their careers, people opting for a simple life style or following vocations with low or variable market returns, or students without grants. (In fact everyone would have the guaranteed income. But, in the middle and upper income groups, it would be netted off against tax.)

Among the nineteenth and early twentieth century Europeans bourgeoisie, a private income was for long a supplement to income for work—and a major cushion and element of flexibility. It enabled people to embark on careers which would not otherwise be possible and to take risks with their careers and lifestyles. European civilisation as it developed from the Renaissance onwards depended on unearned income and inherited wealth. They must indeed play a similar role in the contemporary United States and Japan (e.g. the Kennedys and the Rockefellers); but the lip service paid to the work ethic leads to silence on the matter.

Surely, however, the only thing wrong with unearned income is that too few have it. In all past civilisations the choice was between such income for a few or for none. But if the productive possibilities of robotics and the microprocessor are even a fraction of that claimed for them, the 'modest competence' which was the ideal of the Victorian novelist may eventually be possible for all citizens.

Market-Clearing Pay

There is a fourth argument for Basic Incomes which became especially important with the unemployment explosion of the 1980s. This stems from the argument of market economists that unemployment is due to rates of pay which diverge from market clearing levels.

There are many complicated subtleties and refinements, but they do not obliterate the basic relation between pay and jobs. The problem may lie in excessive money wages or excessive real wages. Or it may lie in the *attempt* to obtain excessive wages, which can only be reconciled with non-accelerating inflation by running the economy at a substantial rate of unemployment. It is also uncertain how far the problem lies with the general wage level and how far it lies with relative wages in different occupations and trades—which would imply that some wages have been too low as well as others too high. All the elements mentioned have played a part—as well as uncertainties about, and sudden shifts in the course of, monetary demand. Fortunately I do not have to apportion relative responsibility here.[3]

None of these complexities undermines the case for market-clearing pay levels. The real difficulty is that market economists too rarely ask: what would or should happen if market-clearing rates of pay for some workers are below the conventional minimum? (They could even be below the physical subsistence level.) In that case they are worse off with a job than on the dole. So even if the unemployed are the opposite of work-shy, they may still find it difficult to take employment.

Basic Incomes would have the effect of topping up the income of low-paid level, so making it possible for workers to price themselves into jobs. An Income Guarantee might admittedly have on (Charles Murray lines) a disincentive effect on those satisfied with the conventional minimum. Such people would be voluntarily unemployed. But everyone will always be better off with a job than without it; and no one will fall below the minimum as a result of taking paid work.

The worry about market-clearing rates of pay being too low to provide acceptable living standards has taken on a new edge because of developments associated with robots and the microchip. They have reawakened the fear that the market-clearing price for many kinds of labour would be extremely low, creating a new kind of poverty in the midst of plenty. Professor Meade was writing eloquently in 1984 of the possibility that new forms of capital equipment might be close and efficient substitutes for labour ('with flexible, intelligent or semi-intelligent powers of receiving, analysing and responding to data') so that, at prevailing wage rates, capital equipment became far more profitable to employ at the margin than labour.

Wages might then fall enough to maintain full employment, but at the expense of a highly concentrated distribution of income 'with the rich owners of robots employing a large number of poorly paid butlers and other servants.' An alternative and more likely result would be that unions would be able to hold up the real wage level for a diminishing employed labour force, while a 'large part of the available workers would have joined the black school leavers from Brixton.'

Meade labels these deliberately 'stark and simple' stories as 'fables'. But his conclusion is that real wages should be allowed to 'change to the extent necessary to provide employment opportunities to all who want them; and this would be possible or tolerable if everyone enjoyed a fair share of the profits earned on the robots, computers and tapes, and indeed on property in general.'

The Basic Income proposal does not depend on the accuracy of the technocratic vision. If robots can really be cheap substitutes for human labour, mass property ownership would turn this development into a great blessing rather than a catastrophe. But such mass share ownership would also make tolerable the distributional effects of the less drastic shift in the relative rewards of labour and capital, which we will need to restore full employment even without science fiction developments.

Indeed we do not have to wait to observe the effect of new technology on the average reward to capital. For we can already in the here and now see an increased dispersion in the market-clearing pay rates for different kinds of workers. Between 1979 and 1986, for instance, the ratio of male real earnings for the bottom tenth of wage earners, relative to those of the average, fell by 20 per cent.

The sad conclusion is that even this relative fall was not sufficient to price all the lowest earners into work. The key problem for European economic and social policy is how to obtain the benefits of a flexible US style labour market, without US poverty or US ghettoes.

A sufficient cut in the dole or a more stringent enforcement of the work-search condition would undoubtedly force many people to find—or create for themselves—more low-paid jobs, of which the extreme example is selling matches at street corners. Thus the pressures would increase on citizens who already face much less attractive conditions than their fellows. That is the danger of the 'workfare' approach. In the US members of the underclass are often the working poor, doing low-paid menial jobs. In Europe where benefit levels are higher, they tend to be the unemployed. Better than either would be a Basic Income Guarantee, which would top up the income of the working poor as well as the unemployed. In that way people with low earning power could take a job without being driven into abject poverty.

The Four Sources of Income

The case for Basic Income is best seen not just as a technical argument among social security experts but as part of a wider ideal under which the responsible citizen has not one, but several sources of income. Professor James Meade has in his book *Agathatopia* listed four such sources:

1. A normal wage or salary;
2. Another part of remuneration from employment which fluctuates in relation to enterprise prosperity;
3. A return on some capital wealth spread over a variety of enterprises; and
4. A tax free social dividend.

This combination of income sources is surely more attractive than pure dependence on wages and would be a feature of any enterprise society worth its name.

The first two sources represent income from employment. The development of a variable component which fluctuates with enterprise prosperity is not a complete novelty. It already exists for instance in the form of sales commissions or partnership incomes. Its extension through Profit Related Pay and other means is an important part of policies to promote employment, but is not a central concern of this Paper. The third and fourth sources represent the return from wealth; obviously so in the case of citizen or employee share holdings, but indirectly so in relation to transfer payments which represent a dividend from general national prosperity.

In public discussion of pay, benefits and related matters there is almost a conspiracy to overlook income not derived from wages and salaries. In 1988 income from work, including self-employment and employers' contributions, accounted for 75 per cent of personal incomes. This still leaves a large remainder, of which 11 per cent was accounted for by rents, dividends and interest, i.e. property incomes, and 14 per cent by social security and related grants.[4] Moreover there is very important income in kind from property, whether the value of owner occupied housing or the amenity value of land, as well as income from household and other unpaid work, not included in the personal income statistics.

The object of these remarks is not to suggest that a big increase in the income of the propertyless would be possible if private capital were expropriated.

About half of all equities are now held by institutions—mainly pension funds—and the proceeds would thus be distributed in large part to those who are now in employment. Any remaining gain from expropriating without compensation would be more than offset by the inefficiencies of state operation and the upheavals resulting from confiscation. My intention is rather to remind readers that the ownership of capital assets need to be put back on the political agenda.

Alternative to Minimum Wage

Basic Income is a superior alternative to the minimum wage ideas which still unfortunately persist on the political Left, and are already in force not only in several European countries but also in the USA. The alternative name for Basic Income 'Minimum Income Guarantee', brings out the contrast with minimum wages more sharply.

Minimum wages represent just that kind of interference with markets which does most harm. Their obvious effect is to price workers out of jobs. The effect is documented in hundreds of studies; and the insistence by minimum wage supporters on further and further proof is like that of those who have to be convinced repeatedly that the earth goes round the sun, and not the other way round. Obviously the size of effect depends on how high the minimum wage is in relation to market-clearing pay, how much variation there is between minima for different types of work, the treatment of part-time work, the opportunities to escape into non-regulated sectors and many other variables. In the US the worst adverse effects have been kept at bay by keeping minimum pay scales low and up-dating them as rarely as possible. The British Labour Party's commitment to an eventual minimum wage of two-thirds the adult average is high enough to be a real danger to employment; and even the commitment to an immediate minimum of one-half the average pay is high enough to do harm to job prospects.

Those most likely to suffer are just the people whom the proponents of minimum wages say they most want to help. They include those on the fringes of the labour market or on the borderline of disablement or other incapacity, the racially disadvantaged, inner city youths, and all the many others who face a choice between low pay and no pay. Minimum wages are a denial of the human right to sell one's labour to a willing buyer and to make one's own decision about whether or not to take paid work at going rates.

Quite apart from the effects on the demand for labour, minimum wages are an extremely inefficient way of helping the poor. Because of divergencies in the number of wage earners and dependents in different households, the link between poverty and pay is much weaker than commonly supposed. Representative studies suggest that only one in five of the poorest 10 per cent of families are in the bottom 10 per cent of the earnings range.[5] A minimum wage, being work related, would be the same for the single bread winner with a large family as for a member of a two earner household without dependents. By contrast, Basic Income varies with family responsibility both in the version where it is paid to individuals and where it is paid to households.

Core Properties

The essence of Basic Income is that everyone receives a basic payment irrespective of all other income. The payment will of course vary with the number of dependents. All additional income is subject to tax.

The idea is that a citizen or household will always receive a Guaranteed Minimum. As earnings rise, more and more is paid in tax, until at the break-even point (B in the chart) the citizen neither pays to, nor receives benefits from the state. At higher incomes he is a net taxpayer. In the pure or ideal scheme, there is no difference between the withdrawal rate of benefit and the tax rate. There is a stable marginal rate of tax throughout.

As an oversimplified and almost certainly over-optimistic illustration, let us assume that the Basic Income is £4,000 per annum with supplements for children. Everyone receives the £4,000 as a tax credit which he or she can offset against his or her tax bill. If he or she has no other earnings he or she will receive the full £4,000. Any further income is taxed at the purely hypothetical rate of 50 per cent. The break-even point where the credit is exhausted—OB on the chart—is reached when earnings from work (or investment income) reach £8,000. Then the tax bill of £4,000 entirely offsets the benefit.

To reduce the cost of the scheme a kink in the tax line may have, for the time being, to be accepted. That is the withdrawal rate of benefit AB, as other income rises towards B, may be steeper than the marginal tax rate BC paid on incomes above the break-even point. Many suggested schemes have a withdrawal rate—such as 80 per cent or more—much higher than the basic rate.

The essential properties of the system are given by three parameters: the size of the tax credit (which is equal to the total benefit received by a person with no other source of income, and is represented by OA); the tax rate (represented by the slope of BC); and the marginal withdrawal rate (if that is different) represented by the slope of AB.[6]

There is no formal reason why there should not be a higher rate of tax on large incomes, leading to a steeper slope on the right of BC. But too many tax bands would complicate both the administration and the understanding of the scheme. If extra impositions on the wealthy are desired (a question left open here) taxes on inheritance, gifts or wealth, while retaining the single income tax, would be more in keeping with the spirit of Basic Incomes.

Figure 1.1 is designed to show the offsetting of tax against benefit. An alternative presentation, designed to show net income levels after tax and benefit is shown in Figure 1.2. The break-even point, where the benefit is exactly offset against tax, is again shown where original income reaches OB. In the hypothetical example, the citizen earns £8,000, receives £4,000 in credit and pays out £4,000 in tax. At that point his net income after tax and benefit is equal to his gross income.

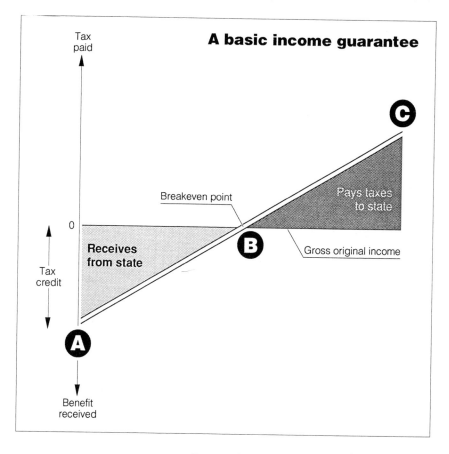

FIGURE 1.1

The essential parameters are once again the size of the tax credit OA and the tax and benefit withdrawal rates. The difference is that a high withdrawal rate is represented by a *shallow* and not a steep slope, as the citizen gains only a modest addition to net income as his gross earnings rise. The diagrams later in this paper, showing specimen Basic Income schemes, are on the lines of Figure 1.2.

Basic Income and Negative Income Tax

The same three parameters can be used to describe a Negative or Reverse Income Tax scheme as well as a Basic Income or Social Dividend scheme. What matters arithmetically is how generous the tax credit is, and how rapidly it is withdrawn and not whether it is called by one name or another.

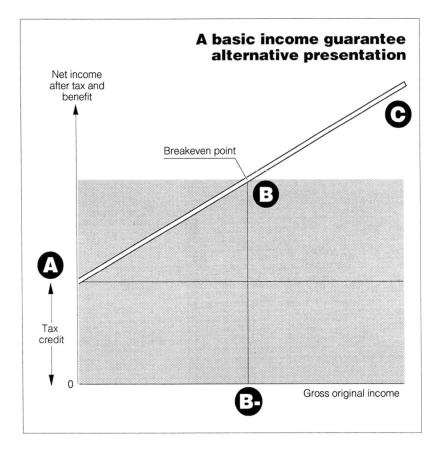

FIGURE 1.2

In any tax and social security system, there are difficult tradeoffs to make between cost, generosity and incentive. The idea of being generous, but concentrating help where it is most needed would be represented by a large initial credit OA and a high withdrawal rate, represented by a steeply sloping AB in Figure 1.1. The problem is that there would be severe disincentive effects of a poverty or unemployment trap kind. If Parliament desires to reduce disincentives by reducing the withdrawal rate, then the scheme becomes far more expensive. If it wishes to keep down *both* the cost and the disincentive effect, then the basic benefit or tax credit would have to be low—and almost certainly inadequate for those with no other source of income.

The integration of tax and social security, however desirable, is an administrative simplification. The three parameters would still have to be chosen. On the other hand the desired result could be achieved even if benefits and tax continued to be paid and collected separately. The difference is that the citizen would have to do his own netting out.

Hermione Parker makes a spirited attempt to show that Basic Income (BI) and Negative Income Tax (NIT) are fundamentally different. The last thing I wish to do is to pick an unnecessary quarrel with Mrs. Parker who has probably done more than any other single individual to keep Basic Income before the public and whose book *Instead of the Dole* is the most comprehensive available treatment of the subject. Disputes about labels and definitions risk polarising the reformers unnecessarily into rival camps.

Mrs Parker's first argument is that Negative Income Tax is less redistributive to the poor than Basic Incomes. This is because Negative Income Tax advocates characteristically advocate a lower basic payment (OA on Figure 1.1) and/or a steeper withdrawal rate (AB) for benefit recipients than the marginal rate of tax (BC). These seem to me to represent differences of degree within the same framework rather than of kind. There can be more or less 'generous' Basic Income or Negative Income Tax schemes. A higher withdrawal rate above the marginal tax rate is acceptable to many Basic Income tax advocates, at least as a necessary evil until the fully fledged scheme can be introduced. The differences are along a continuum rather than between incompatible proposals.

A second fundamental difference mentioned by Mrs Parker is that NIT takes the household as the unit and BI takes the individual. There is no reason why this must be so. Indeed some supporters of NIT have in mind individuals and some BI supporters think of households, at least provisionally. The issue is discussed in more detail in Steven Webb's chapters, and especially in his Appendix.

The third difference is administrative. A Basic Income is paid out regularly every month or week. The procedure is more helpful to those on low or fluctuating incomes, or who have difficulties with the bureaucratic machine, than belated attempts by tax authorities to adjust for changing circumstances. For this reason, earlier BI supporters accepted 'churning' under which most citizens both receive the Basic Income and pay tax. But Mrs Parker stresses that this is no longer necessary with modern computer methods, and she herself emphasises the benefits of integrating tax and benefits, referring to both schools of thought as members of the 'integrationist' camp. The fact that she, like other BI supporters, finds relevant evidence in American NIT experiments, shows how interrelated the ideas are.

Notes

1 House of Commons Social Services Committee, 1989. *Social Security, Changes Implemented in April 1988*, Session 1988–89.
2 A fuller explanation is given in S. Brittan, (1988) Chapter 3.
3 For further discussion, see Brittan (1988), pp. 282–301.
4 UK National Accounts. There is an element of double counting in these estimates, as benefits are financed by taxes on the other sources of income.
5 Richard Layard, *More Jobs, Less Inflation*, Grant McIntyre, 1982.
6 This presentation owes a great deal to A R Prest and N Barr, (1986).

2 Wider Aspects

Samuel Brittan

Preconditions

To the extent that a Basic Income provides cash to those who do not obtain it from the present Welfare State, it has a resource cost. The cost must be in the shape of either higher taxes or tax cuts not made. To pretend otherwise is self-deception. The only way of easing the cost is for the national income to grow faster than the acceptable size of the Basic Income.

Would a Basic Income make a national output grow more or less quickly? It is impossible to say *a priori*. Some people now unemployed or out of the labour force would respond by taking lower paid or part-time or intermittent jobs. There would also be less stigma attached to employers who offered such jobs, as they would know that pay would be topped up by income transfers and workers would be able to afford to take them. Thus wages would be even lower in some low-paid jobs than they are at present. But *standards of living* at the bottom would not suffer. For all that would happen is that workers with earning power near the conventional minimum could receive pay rather than the dole, raising employment and national income levels.

But as against this favourable effect, there would be two unfavourable effects. As the marginal tax rate would be higher with a Basic Income than without it, the usual disincentive effects to increased earnings would apply. Their presence makes it all the more important to have a single basic tax rate and not to worsen incentives by superimposing higher rates in the middle or upper income range. Secondly, while it will never be unprofitable to take a job, the replacement ratio (income out of work divided by potential net income in employment) will be increased for many people, simply as a result of the higher tax-take. Thus some workers may drop out of the labour force altogether. There is some mitigation from the fact that those most likely to do so are part-timers, many of them women, who earn too little to contribute much to tax revenue under the present regime. It is impossible to say *a priori* which effects will be strongest. But the nearer that Minimum Income is to median or average earnings, the more likely are the disincentive effects to prevail—and more in proportion as the gap is narrowed.[1]

Thus the essential condition for affordability is that there should be a distinct and growing gap between national income per head and the target minimum. It was the lack of such a gap which destroyed the primitive experiment in Guaranteed Basic Incomes at the beginning of the nineteenth century, known as Speenhamland. (The Speenhamland System named after a meeting of magistrates in a place of that name in Berkshire in 1795, made up from parish rates deficiencies in labourers' income below agreed rates. It was widely condemned for encouraging both idleness and low wages and was superseded by the more severe 1834 Poor Law.)

A fully fledged Basic Income will thus only be possible if it is accepted that poverty and the tolerable minimum income are not just relative concepts. There is no need to go to the other extreme and exclude any conventional element. Assume a doubling of average real incomes over a period; and consider a relatively poor person whose income also doubles from, say, £4,000 per annum to £8,000 per annum, but who still earns only one-third of national pay. It does have to be accepted that the poorer person is better off—not necessarily twice as well off, but better off—than before. If we insist on a purely relative definition of poverty then we shall perpetuate for all time the state of affairs of the late 1980s where 140 per cent of the Income Support level for a family with three children took a single breadwinner to 86 per cent of average national pay.

The Thatcher Government's decision to link benefit levels to inflation rather than earnings will in time enlarge the gap between benefit and pay. The process will continue even if there are occasional real benefit upratings, or there is an alternation between governments linking benefits to earnings and those linking them to prices only. The essential condition is that the gap grows, however spasmodically.

Finding Resources

Suggestions for 'finding the money' for a Basic Income, are worth attention as ways of reducing the pain of transfer. But they do not create resources out of thin air.

One idea, suggested by Hermione Parker, is that resources should be found by phasing out mortgage interest relief and tax relief on pension fund contributions. (A property or site value tax might be an alternative to the former measure.) The phasing out of special interest privileges always deserves a cheer (even when they run counter to the reforms advocated by the 'expenditure tax' lobby). Tax allowances related to specific expenditure would in effect be exchanged for unconditional tax credits—which is what Basic Income would be for most people at work. Nevertheless, there would still have to be an increase in the overall tax burden.

Early advocates of Negative Tax placed high hopes on cash payments to individuals replacing the need for social services in kind, such as health and education. These hopes were never realistic. For if the payments were to be large enough to replace state expenditure on health and education, they would have to be very large indeed.

Even if we abandon as a chimera the hopes of saving money through a switch to self-provision what are the prospects on their own merits? Not very bright, I am afraid. Due to the economic characteristics of insurance,[2] privatisation is unlikely to provide effective or adequate health care. I am not persuaded that such objections apply to anything like the same extent to primary or secondary education. But I am impressed by how entrenched state finance for schooling, if not actual provision, is throughout the world. The effects of ill-thought out attempts at reform can be to increase the power of central government at the expense of pupils and parents alike.

It is because they have realised that integrating tax and Social Security (with or without commuting social services in kind) does not offer an easy way of reducing the cost of the Welfare State that many members of the Radical Right have now gone off the Negative Income Tax idea altogether. Instead they now increasingly realise that the first effects of integrating tax and Social Security would be to reveal some of the gaps in existing anti-poverty policy and thus lead to a demand for more expenditure rather than less.

The area where lower state involvement could facilitate Basic Income would be in housing. So long as housing costs vary so widely for reasons whch have little to do with quality or quantity of accommodation, many poor families are going to need the additional top-up of Housing Benefit, despite its selective and means tested aspects. The freer the housing market becomes, the easier will it be to phase out at least part of Housing Benefit and convert it into a larger Basic Income instead.

Capital Endowment

A different kind of idea put forward by Professor James Meade (1989) is that instead of aiming for a balanced Budget, to which the UK Government is committed, the Budget surplus which emerged at the end of the 1980s should be preserved and even enhanced.

Enthusiasts for fiscal policy will claim that Budget surpluses will not only transfer resources, but make a Basic Income more affordable by raising national savings and the growth of national output. I do not believe this, because I fear that most or all of the increase in public savings would be offset by lower private savings, as we have already seen. But to argue the matter further would take us too far away from the main theme. Basic Income advocates can still argue for Budget surpluses as a transfer mechanism without being optimistic about their effects on the national growth rate.

If Budget surpluses are maintained for long enough, not only will the National Debt eventually be extinguished, but the state will become a net holder of financial assets. Thus interest on the National Debt, now running at around £17 billion per annum, will be eliminated. Eventually the state will start accumulating assets from which it will receive net income.

A policy of raising revenue to extinguish the National Debt and provide the state with financial assets is equivalent to a very gradual and non-disruptive capital levy, designed to provide an endowment for those who would have otherwise little or no capital. This can be seen if it is assumed for illustration that the state buys private sector bonds. These are debts by companies, and are thus a subtraction from private sector wealth. This way of putting it emphasises that one aim of the Basic Income scheme is to offset the very skewed distribution of capital ownership which is one of the less desirable features of capitalism.

What form, however, should government financial assets take? They could not literally be bonds, as bond finance is not important for British companies, partly because of high and uncertain nominal interest rates. The public authorities could buy commercial bills, as they did earlier in the 1980s when they accumulated a bill mountain in their attempts to massage downwards the monetary aggregates. But there are limits to such possibilities. The effects on the structure of interest rates (depressing short term rates relative to long term ones) may not always be desirable; the supply of bills may run out; and the implications of the corporate sector being heavily indebted to government need more attention than they are given by the champions of overfunding.

One alternative might be for the Government to invest any surpluses overseas so that the official British stake would be too small to be decisive anywhere. Here, too, there would have to be a self-denying ordinance not to try to purchase political or economic influence by carefully chosen placements. The experience of the Kuwait Investment Office has shown how difficult it is to avoid international complications, even when there is a genuine desire to treat the funds purely as investments.

Meade's own idea is that the state should eventually acquire a 50 per cent stake in the real assets of the community. It would not attempt a managerial function, but would put its stake in investment trusts and similar institutions where its funds would be merged with private funds in search of the highest yield. In contrast to post-war nationalisation, the Meade form—which he himself calls 'topsy turvey'—would be to take over the yield on state-owned equity, but leave management in private, competitive hands. But without going into further details, it is simply not credible that a government of any political persusasion could own 50 per cent of the national business capital and then observe a self-denying ordinance not to meddle. It is not even likely that the yield from these assets will be used exclusively to finance the Basic Income.

A better procedure might be to hand over the assets purchased to trustees, who would have the duty of grouping them into bundles of convenient size, prior to distributing them to individual citizens on a pro rata or other very simple basis. There would be positive advantages in a minimum income for all, that was seen to be derived even partly from a stake in the nation's capital by all citizens, and not a handout from the Social Security system.

The Basic Income concept belongs to the same family of ideas as wider capital ownership. In 1978 I suggested that the incomes from the state's stake in North Sea oil should be handed over to individual citizens, the rights to which could be realised in the capital market. Later on in 1984 I suggested that privatised shares should be handed over 'free' to citizens instead of being sold (in very expensive manner with high overheads) to private investors. (The nearest the later idea came to realisation was privatisation sales at slightly below market prices with baits for the small investor. This has introduced a larger minority to share ownership, but at a high cost to the Exchequer, and without reversing the drift of share ownership to the institutions.)

Basic Income payments financed by transfers of capital assets would be a device of a like nature. There would be a dilemma in determining what the citizens could do with their new assets. If there were no limits on realisation, they would be very much like normal equity ownership, but there would be the danger that some people would sell these holdings and not have a minimum income. Restrictions on realisation would reduce this danger but also make the holdings less like citizens' capital. The analogy between a state-provided minimum scheme and the capital holdings which provide the bourgeois with investment income, like all analogies, is thus not a complete one; and a choice of advantages would have to be made.

An examination of the economics of over-repayment of the National Debt is useful in bringing out some of the linkages between Basic Incomes and capital ownership. But to get anywhere near achieving it, successive governments would have to stand firm against all pressures from the left and centre for an increase in the growth of public spending, including pressures from active supporters of Basic Income. They would also have to stand firm against pressures from the right for the use of Budget surpluses to finance straightforward tax cuts. Realistically, the prospects of a series of Budget surpluses enough to more than repay the National Debt is so remote that I lose no sleep over the resulting problems. We should be lucky if the UK Budget achieves over a run of years a balance not dependent on privatisation or other asset sales.

Notes

1 See Meade (1989), Appendix 2.
2 See Barr (1987), especially Chapters 5 and 12.

3 The UK Direct Tax and Social Security Systems: Key Facts

Steven Webb

Chapter Four describes some feasibility studies of the way in which the social security and tax systems could be modified in the direction of providing a guaranteed income for all and then draws some conclusions. But before doing so, it will be helpful to set out briefly some details of the present system, both as it stands at the time of writing and as it is likely to develop over coming years.

Social Security

Social Security is by far the largest single item of Government expenditure, costing £56bn in 1990–91 or around 30 per cent of total Government spending. Within this total we may identify three main areas of expenditure.

a) National Insurance benefits
b) Income-related benefits
c) Other contingent benefits.

Table 3.1 shows expenditure on social security in 1990–91, subdivided in this way.

a) National Insurance benefits

The most important single group of benefits is National Insurance benefits which together account for half of all social security spending. The main NI benefits are the retirement pension, unemployment benefit, invalidity and sickness benefits, and the widows' pension, and of these the retirement pension is by far the most significant in terms of expenditure. Entitlement to these benefits depends on an individual's record of National Insurance Contributions over a specified period and does not vary with current income. Those who have made the requisite number of contributions over the relevant period are entitled to the basic amount of the benefit together with a smaller addition for any dependent adult. In the case of the long term

17

benefits such as retirement pension or widows' pension, those with an inadequate record of contributions may be entitled to a reduced amount of benefit. The principal rates of National Insurance benefits in 1990–91 are shown in Table 3.2.[1]

TABLE 3.1 SOCIAL SECURITY EXPENDITURE PLANS 1990–91

National Insurance Benefits	(£ million)
Retirement Pension	23,000
Invalidity Benefit	4,500
Unemployment Benefit	1,000
Widows' Benefits	1,000
Sickness Benefit / SSP	1,200
Other	900
Total NI Benefits	31,600
Income—Related Benefits	
Income Support[a]	8,700
Housing Benefit[b] / Community Charge Rebate	3,500
Family Credit	500
Total Income—Related	12,700
Other Contingent Benefits	
Child Benefit / One Parent Benefit	4,800
Attendance Allowance	1,400
Mobility Allowance	900
War Pensions	700
Other	700
Total Other Contingent	8,500
Administration	2,800
Total Social Security	55,600

[a]Including Social Fund
[b]Excludes rent rebates (England and Wales) of £2.4 bn now administered by the Department of Environment.
SOURCE: Public Expenditure White Paper 1990, Vol 15. Social Security

TABLE 3.2. RATES OF PRINCIPAL NATIONAL INSURANCE BENEFITS (£ P.W.)

	Basic amount	addition for dependent adult
Retirement pension	46.90	28.20
Widows' pension	46.90	—
Unemployment benefit	37.35	23.05
Sickness benefit	35.70	22.10

It is important to note that, of the short term NI benefits for those under pension age, only widow's benefit has additions for dependent children. Families with children where the head is unemployed or sick may well be entitled to claim an income-related benefit as well as the relevant National Insurance benefit.

b) Income-related benefits

The three most important income-related benefits are Income Support (formerly supplementary benefit), Family Credit, and Housing benefit and together these account for around one-quarter of social security spending.

Income Support is available to those not in full-time work, and is designed to bring family incomes up to a minimum level whose precise value depends on family size and composition. Where the claimant has any other income (such as National Insurance benefits, small amounts of earnings etc.) this is withdrawn pound-for-pound from Income Support entitlement.

Family Credit is a much smaller benefit, designed to supplement the incomes of low income working families with children. A maximum credit depending on family size is payable to those whose income after tax and National Insurance falls below a specified threshold. Where income rises above this level, Family Credit is reduced by 70 pence for every extra pound of income.

Housing Benefit is available to all those on low incomes to provide help in paying rent and (now only in N.Ireland) domestic rates. For the rest of the UK a Community Charge benefit operates along similar lines. Recipients of income support have all of their rent paid and 80 per cent of any domestic rates/community charge. For those with incomes (after tax and National Insurance) above the Income Support level, rent rebate is withdrawn at the rate of 65p in the pound and Community Charge rebate at the rate of 15p in the pound. A common feature of these income-related benefits is that those with capital in excess of a specified ceiling (currently £8,000 for Income Support and Family Credit, £8,000 for rent rebates and £18,000 for Community Charge benefit) are disqualified from receiving any of the benefits. The principal rates of Income Support and Family Credit are shown in Table. 3.3.

One structural problem associated with these benefits and with family credit in particular is that of non-take-up. In each case the numbers actually claiming the benefit in question fall well short of the numbers estimated to be entitled, and at an aggregate level large amounts of money go unclaimed. Thus in the case of Family Credit, latest estimates suggest that only half of these who are entitled to the benefit take up their entitlement, and only around two-thirds of available expenditure on the benefit is actually claimed. The figures for housing benefits and income support are rather better, but take-up rates of around 85 per cent by numbers are the best that have been achieved with benefits of this kind *administered in the present way*. The importance of this issue is discussed in more detail later.

c) Other contingent benefits

This residual category contains a wide range of benefits where entitlement is not related to National Insurance Contributions nor does it vary with income. To qualify for one of the benefits in this category a claimant must simply satisfy a particular 'contingency' such as having children or suffering from a particular disability. The main benefits in this category are Child Benefit and long term sickness benefits such as Mobility Allowance and Attendance Allowance.

Child benefit is payable at a flat rate for each child and the amount payable does not depend on income. Child Benefit is currently £7.25 per week and has not been increased since April 1987. An additional payment, currently £5.60 per week, is payable to all lone parents.

These then are the principal elements of the UK social security system. We now consider the personal direct tax system, considering in turn income tax, National Insurance contributions, and finally the Community Charge.

TABLE 3.3. RATES OF INCOME SUPPORT AND FAMILY CREDIT 1990–91

Income support	(£ per week)
—Personal allowances	
married couple	57.60
single (age 25 +)	36.70
single (age 18–24)	28.80
child: aged 0–10	12.35
child: aged 11–15	18.25
child: aged 16–17	21.90
child: aged 18	28.80
—Premiums	
family[a]	7.35
lone parent	4.10
couple pensioner (60–74)	17.95
single pensioner (60–74)	11.80
Family Credit	
— Credits	
adult[b]	36.35
child 16–17	17.80
11–15	14.15
0–10	8.25
—Income threshold	57.60

[a]Available on first child.
[b]One adult credit is available per family.

Note. For Housing benefit, the claimant's income is compared with his income support needs level, and any excess is deducted from maximum assistance with rent and community charge in the manner described above.

Personal direct taxes in the UK

a) Income Tax

Income tax is the largest single source of Government revenue accounting for around one-quarter of revenues in 1990–91. A wide range of sources of personal income including earnings. self-employment income, investment income and certain National Insurance benefits are subject to income tax. The total of income subject to tax may however be reduced by the use of personal allowances. The value of these allowances is shown in Table 3.4. (Higher allowances are available for those over pension age).

TABLE 3.4. INCOME TAX ALLOWANCES 1990–91

	(£ p.a.)
Married couple's allowance[1]	1720
Personal allowance	3005

[1] This allowance may be used by one partner in a married couple

Once taxable income after allowances has been calculated, further deductions may be made for allowable expenditures such as mortgage interest payments and contributions into pension schemes. The revenue costs of these two deductions are estimated at £7bn. and £5bn. respectively for 1989–90. The final figure for taxable income is then used to assess income tax liability according to the schedule of rates and bands shown in Table 3.5. The effect of a wide basic rate band together with a range of allowances and deductions means that the vast majority of taxpayers will pay tax at the basic rate.

TABLE 3.5. INCOME TAX RATES AND BANDS 1990–91

Range of taxable income	rate (%)
0–20,700	25
20,701 and over	40

b) National Insurance Contribution

National Insurance Contributions (NICs) are levied on employees, employers and the self-employed and have in recent years become an increasingly important source of Government revenue. In 1990–91 NIC revenues will be around £36 bn, or around three-fifths of the revenue from income tax. NICs are levied on earned income only, with employees earning below a 'Lower Earnings Limit' being exempt from NICs, and those earning above an 'Upper Earnings Limit' paying no further NICs on income in excess of that amount. Those earning above the Lower Earnings Limit pay employee NICs of 2 per cent on earnings up to the LEL and then 9 per cent on any excess up to the Upper Earnings Limit. The 9% rate may be reduced to 7% for those who choose to "contract out" of the State Earnings-Related Pension Scheme (SERPS) and make contributions instead into a personal or occupational scheme. The current lower and upper earnings limits for employee NICs are shown in Table 6.

TABLE 3.6. EMPLOYEE NICS EARNINGS LIMITS 1990–91

	(£ p.w.)
Lower	46
Upper	350

The system of employer contributions is far more complex, but perhaps the most inportant single difference is that there is no upper limit or 'ceiling' on the earnings on which employer NICs may be levied. As with employee NICs, a reduced rate of contribution is payable by an employer in respect of a 'contracted out' employee. In 1988–89 the revenues from employer and employee NICs were broadly comparable, but in 1989–90 and beyond it is likely that employer NICs will become more important relative to employee NICs.

c) Community Charge

Around one-quarter of local authority revenue in England, Wales and Scotland comes from an individual-based Community Charge. The amount of Community Charge payable does not depend upon the taxpayer's income, although a rebate system similar to the rate rebate system operated under the Housing Benefit scheme operates for those on lower incomes. The maximum rebate will be 80 per cent of the Community Charge, and as income rises above income support levels, rebate is reduced by 15 pence in the pound. The simulations which follow are based on the tax and benefit system prior to the full introduction of the Community Charge. They are thus based on the old system of domestic rates, a property-based tax levied on households. The inclusion of community charge rebates rather than rate rebates does not, however, significantly affect the argument.

This section has provided no more than an outline of the principal personal direct taxes and social security benefits in the UK. In the next section I consider some of the shortcomings of that system and examine some proposals for reform.

Note

1 Since the early 1980s, these benefits have typically been uprated annually in line with prices.

4 Some Illustrative Schemes

Steven Webb

Introduction and summary

In popular debate, the UK social security system is often characterised as acting as a 'safety net'. This image suggests that there is a certain level of income—usually supposed to be the income support line—below which individuals are not allowed to fall without the state stepping in. In fact, there are a number of reasons, discussed in this section, why this is an oversimplification, and why some individuals may well find themselves with incomes below the income support line. Official figures (see DSS 1988b) back up this view, showing that in 1985 there were 2.4 million family units with incomes below the supplementary benefit line. Although such figures should be treated with caution (see DSS 1988a) they do seem to indicate that a large number of citizens are not in fact guaranteed a minimum income by the state. Furthermore, these figures are silent on the issue of within-family poverty. The possibility that there may be genuinely poor individuals within even relatively affluent families is one which has received increasing attention of late and to which we return later.

Given that this is the case, what then would be required for the state to be effectively guaranteeing a basic income to all? It seems clear that what would be required is far more than a minor extension of the existing system. The problems of non-take-up (discussed below) are inherent in the mechanisms by which benefits are paid and will not be solved simply by more advertising campaigns. Extending coverage of benefits to new groups without changing the method of delivery would suffer from the same drawback. Similarly, restrictions of benefits to those who are not seen as the 'deserving poor' (e.g. those who are 'voluntarily' unemployed) reflect fundamental attitudes towards the provision of state income support. It is clear that if the objective is to be a guaranteed basic income then radical changes are needed in the UK tax and social security system, and in the philosophy which underlies it.

In the remainder of this section I discuss a three stage progression towards such a system. I begin by outlining the principal defects of the present system in failing to lift substantial numbers of families even to the income support/supplementary benefit level, and move on to consider what a guaranteed basic income scheme might look like. I then examine the

23

arguments for and against a radical reshaping of the present system to provide such a scheme. Finally some detailed simulations are presented which examine the cost and effects of various reform options which might go some or all of the way towards guaranteeing a basic income to all.

It should be noted at the outset that the simulations presented in this section are based on a model of the UK tax and benefit system as it stood in Autumn 1989, that is, prior to the introduction of independent taxation. In general, the redistributional effects of the transition will be relatively minor, and so this change will not affect the general principles illustrated by the various schemes.

Does the UK Social Security System Provide a Guaranteed Basic Income?

As noted at the outset, there are a number of reasons why the present social security system fails to guarantee that the income of all families will reach even the basic income support level. We discuss the principal reasons below.

i) Incomplete coverage

Whilst social security benefits such as income support (IS) exist for those not in full-time work, and there is also the family credit (FC) scheme for full-time workers with children, there is no benefit to assist with the normal living expenses (apart from housing costs) of childless working families. It is thus quite possible that the net income of a childless working family may fall below the income support line, and no state income supplement would be available.

ii) Incomplete take-up

Owing to the mechanism by which income-related benefits are delivered, there is no guarantee that even those who do fall within a group covered by the benefits system will actually claim and receive such benefits. Whether this is due to ignorance of the existence of the benefit, costs of claiming, feelings of stigma or whatever, non-take-up remains an important source of gaps in the social security system.[1] The problem is particularly acute in the case of family credit, where around half of those who are entitled to the benefit do not claim it, with a third of the money available going unclaimed. The Government's own statistics (see DSS 1988b) suggest that it was a combination of these two factors—non-take-up and incomplete coverage—which left 240,000 full-time workers with net incomes below the supplementary benefit line in 1985.

iii) Disqualifications

Even where an individual falls into a category covered by the benefit system, and where benefit is actually claimed, state support is only provided in full subject to certain conditions. These include requirements (in the case of income support) that unemployed claimants be actively seeking work, that any unemployment was not voluntary, and for other claimants that they are not involved in an industrial dispute. Claimants are also disqualified from receipt of income-related benefits if they have capital in excess of certain limits. Where these conditions are not met, benefit may be withheld or paid only in part and so there is again no guarantee of a state-funded basic income for these groups.

As already mentioned even where benefits or wages are reaching families at an adequate level, they may not be benefiting all individuals within the family equally. This possibility will be important in determining the unit over which entitlement to benefit is assessed. I discuss this issue more fully in Appendix 1.

For all of these reasons it is clearly misleading to regard the present social security system as providing a guaranteed basic income to all families, let alone to all individuals. Furthermore, the direction of recent policy has been away from providing universal benefits and towards 'targeting' of benefits through the use of means-testing. Thus the universal Child Benefit, which has many of the features of a basic income payment, has been frozen for three years, whilst some of the resources thereby released have been channelled into the means-tested family credit. Similarly, the basic National Insurance retirement pension has been uprated only in line with prices rather than earnings throughout the 1980s, whilst at the same time means-tested benefits for older pensioners have been made somewhat more generous. In addition, the rules for entitlement to National Insurance benefits and to means-tested benefits have been steadily tightened over the last ten years, providing little encouragement for those who would wish to see a move towards unconditional basic incomes paid as of right.

The next section considers what sort of system would be required to produce a genuinely guaranteed income for all.

What does a Guaranteed Basic Income Scheme look like?

Before discussing the general merits and limitations of a guaranteed basic income scheme we should consider what such a scheme might look like.

Considering first the notion of an income guarantee, some consideration must be given to the way in which the guarantee is to be fulfilled. Under the present system the onus is very much on the individual both to be aware of and to claim the benefits. Partly as a result of this feature, only around one-half of low income families with children claim their family credit entitlement. It would thus be difficult to defend the claim that low income working families, for example, are guaranteed a basic income.

Where, however, methods of claiming are simple (or indeed 'claiming' is unnecessary), where the value of the benefit is more stable and where the coverage of the benefit is more comprehensive, then something more like a guarantee might be achieved. One benefit in the present system which fits this description is Child Benefit whose take-up rate is close to 100 per cent. Clearly if any reform option is to be described as an income guarantee it must possess many of these features.

In the light of this, a distinguishing feature of almost all proposals for an income guarantee is the notion of universality. Here the aim is that the income guarantee is seen as a right of all rather than as a concession to an unfortunate few. The schemes proposed typically apply a single system to most, if not all of the population, with a minimum of exceptions. Because a single system of assessment is applied to all, the distinction between 'claimants' who depend on the state scheme, and taxpayers who finance it may become less acute.

A further element of any scheme which must be defined is what sort of 'basic' income is being guaranteed. Is it to be a subsistence level, or one which allows the individual/family to enjoy a more active role in society? Simply because of the cost of such schemes, particularly when based on the individual, attention has typically focused on schemes which at most provide what an affluent society would regard as no more than a subsistence income. In this paper we follow this tradition, and examine a scheme which would eventually guarantee to all families an income equal to the present income support line.

Income guarantee schemes will often involve a major redistribution of income, and the mechanism by which income is to be transferred must also be specified. A common feature of most proposed schemes is to integrate rates of withdrawal of the various benefits into the income tax mechanism. However, since most income-related benefits are currently withdrawn very rapidly as income rises[2] then the combined rate of withdrawal must reflect this if the scheme is to be affordable. Some proposed schemes thus involve a uniform withdrawal rate which is lower than these benefit withdrawal rates but significantly higher than the current income tax rate. Others concentrate very high marginal tax rates on those on lower incomes and have a lower withdrawal rate for the rest of the population.

Whichever option is chosen, the greater coverage of guaranteed income schemes will increase their cost relative to the present system and thus increase the rates of tax necessary to pay for them. Furthermore, since basic income schemes often involve the abolition of most tax allowances, these higher rates will often apply as soon as a few pounds have been earned. This may have major implications for work incentives, especially for secondary earners who can currently earn at least £57 per week without paying tax.

I have considered then some of the issues raised by the notion of a guaranteed basic income, together with the ways in which they are typically dealt with in the actual schemes which have been proposed. I now move on to consider the arguments for and against schemes of this general kind.

Is a Guaranteed Basic Income Desirable?

A wide range of arguments had been presented in favour of some sort of state-guaranteed basic income. Although the discussion has centred so far on poverty prevention, a number of other social, economic and moral justifications have been advanced. This section discusses some of the principal arguments, together with some possible criticisms. (A more extensive discussion of the arguments for and against a basic income scheme is contained in Walter 1989).

Perhaps the most obvious advantage of a *guaranteed* basic income scheme would be the relief of poverty. Quite simply, if individuals automatically receive a basic income from the state as a right, rather than having to be aware of and claim certain benefits and fulfil certain requirements as at present, then there will be far fewer poor people. In the first place the problem of take-up is likely to be significantly reduced or eliminated, depending on the specific administrative mechanism chosen. Secondly, the universal nature of the payment would mean that no group (such as childless working families as at present) would be excluded. Thirdly, such schemes would typically do away with disqualifications on the grounds of 'non-availability for work', too much capital and so on, and would thus fill gaps in the present system.

Apart from purely financial considerations, income guarantee schemes have also been justified on the grounds that they improve the dignity and social standing of what is currently the benefit receiving population. Again this is an area where merely tinkering with the present system would achieve relatively little. Perhaps the best way to guarantee that all receive a minimum income is to assess the tax/benefit position of all families using a single mechanism rather than having a separate system for benefit claimants and for taxpayers. This is a feature of most proposals aiming to provide a guaranteed basic income.

It is possible of course that a new division might be created between those who 'earn' their income, and those who actively choose merely to subsist on the basic state income. The political acceptability of such a scheme might depend on whether the main beneficiaries were those popularly conceived of as being the 'deserving' poor. In the longer term however, the presence of a guaranteed source of unearned income might itself begin to change attitudes to work and leisure.

State guaranteed basic income schemes have also been justified on the grounds of a right to share in the prosperity of society as a whole. This approach, in the 'social dividend' tradition (see for example Rhys-Williams 1942) argues that prosperity results not solely from individual effort but more from the endowed technology and resources of the society, and that these benefits should be shared fairly. Such a perspective might be particularly appropriate in an era where the number of individuals involved in productive activity may decline and where rewards might otherwise be concentrated very heavily in the hands of a highly productive and privileged few.

This approach does however highlight what many see as a fundamental weakness of income guarantee schemes, namely that they might discourage enterprise and work effort. This could arise for two reasons. Firstly, many income guarantee schemes would increase the ratio of incomes when out of work to incomes when in work (the 'replacement ratio') and might thus discourage some individuals from taking low paid work. Secondly, since many minimum income schemes require that all other income should be taxed in full then the incentives for secondary earners in particular may be worsened. They will no longer be able to earn around £57 p.w. before paying tax but will instead be paying tax (at a rate probably well in excess of the current basic rate) on the first pound that is earned. This latter effect would arise only if the scheme concerned involved the scrapping of tax allowances as a revenue raising measure, but this is not a necessary feature of an income guarantee scheme.

Not only may it be undesirable to discourage work in this way, but such an outcome could also threaten the finances of an income guarantee scheme. If many were to withdraw from the labour force, tax revenues would fall creating the need for higher taxes from those remaining in the labour force. These in turn might discourage others from remaining in the labour force and so the process could continue.

In practice, however, the argument of ever-declining participation requiring ever-increasing taxes to be paid by the remaining participants may not be very likely. The group whose labour supply is most responsive to changes in the tax and benefit system is married women, and within this group it would be part-timers who would be most affected. Because of the operation of the tax allowance, such women typically pay relatively little in income tax. Whilst it is debatable whether one would wish to discourage such women from working, their non-participation would be unlikely to create a major dent in the finances of an income guarantee scheme.

It has also been argued that a comprehensive income guarantee scheme could in fact generate new jobs which would not be created under the present system. As Samuel Brittan has noted in Chapter 1, under the operation of a free market in labour, there is no guarantee that the market clearing wage will reach subsistence levels. If the wage being offered were below such a level then there would be no incentive to take such a job under the present income support scheme. Any income earned thereby would simply be withdrawn pound for pound from benefit entitlement. In the presence of a guaranteed basic income however, there would still be a (small) net financial benefit in taking such a job. Thus an income guarantee scheme might in fact generate new jobs and draw some individuals back in to the labour market.

The main feature of most income guarantee schemes which would make such an outcome possible is that as well as guaranteeing a minimum income, they also typically incorporate a rate of tax on other income which is always less than 100 per cent. It is this which creates a net financial gain from taking any paid employment. It is interesting to note that a similar result would be achievable within the present system if the rate of withdrawal of income support were to be reduced below 100 per cent. Such a change is, however, unlikely given the philosophy on which the present benefit system is based.

It has also been argued that an unconditional guaranteed minimum income could provide a springboard for enterprise and a flexibility in the labour market. On enterprise, the minimum income could provide a secure floor which would encourage risk-taking and could possibly replace the current rather complex web of schemes to encourage small businesses and the self-employed.

Flexibility with regard to labour market participation over a lifetime might also be enhanced by the presence of a state guaranteed minimum income. If it were possible to leave the labour market without prejudicing future benefit receipt (currently a problem because of the National Insurance system) then freer movement in and out of paid employment would become feasible. This might enhance opportunities for further education or training, or might encourage the wider introduction of job-sharing schemes.

As this brief survey suggests, a range of justifications had been advanced for the introduction of a guaranteed minimum income scheme. Some possible objections have been mentioned above, including disincentive effects and a concern that the quite radical shift to a guaranteed unearned income for all might prove difficult politically. However, this debate is all in vain if a guaranteed minimum income is simply not affordable. In the remainder of this chapter we thus focus our attention on the specific issue of the cost of a minimum income guarantee.

Is a guaranteed minimum income affordable?

Most proposed schemes for providing a guaranteed basic income are based on the individual. Regardless of the earnings of any partner, each individual is still entitled to the full basic income payment, and consequently such schemes are potentially very expensive. Even proponents of these schemes acknowledge that the rates of tax needed to finance payments at adequate levels would be prohibitive. (Parker (1988) has suggested that a uniform marginal tax rate of 70–85 per cent might be required for a scheme guaranteeing 'adequate' incomes to all individuals.)

One response to this, which Parker has taken, is to propose partial basic income schemes. In these schemes the unconditionality and individual basis of the payments is maintained, but they are made at a level which is not sufficient on its own for subsistence. Income related supplements are then made available to assist those families whose incomes fall below specified levels. A variety of such schemes is set out in detail in Parker (1988).

However, an alternative approach, which seeks to retain some of the benefits of income guarantee schemes but at an affordable cost, is to pay guaranteed minimum incomes to all family units rather than to all individuals. Clearly such an approach does nothing to solve problems of intra-family distribution and dependency, but it does represent a more natural extension of the present system where income-related social security benefits are similarly based on the family unit. It is also a far cheaper approach since no income supplement need be paid if one partner has sufficient income for the whole family.

In this section three stages are examined by which one could move from the present social security system to a family based income guarantee scheme. I consider first a relatively minor change, namely the extension of family credit (as presently operated) to all full-timers, whether or not they have children. This would at least ensure that childless full-timers whose incomes fell below the income support line had the possibility of a state income supplement. This relatively modest scheme would not however solve the problem of non-take-up, a problem which besets family credit in particular. For all but low earners, this reform would have no net effect.

Next a more radical reform is considered of the tax and benefit system as it affects full-time workers. This would involve the payment of full family credit to all full-timers (regardless of income), with the additional benefit being financed by a higher rate of income tax. Since all full-timers would be entitled to the full family credit irrespective of income, take-up should be significantly improved. This scheme would in effect guarantee a minimum income to all families where one person is working full time.

Finally, this approach is extended to a reform involving the whole population. Under our third scheme, all families would receive unconditionally a full level of benefit regardless of income. This overall payment from the state would be equal to the current income support levels and would take the place of both income support and family credit. Those whose National Insurance benefits brought them close to existing Income Support levels would receive only a small supplement so that the overall state payment was equal to the Income Support level. This universal payment would then be financed by a higher overall rate of income tax charged on all other income (above a small allowance).

Each is considered in turn.

i) Extended Family Credit

As noted at the outset, one group which can fall below subsistence levels because it is not catered for by the income-related benefit system is childless full-time workers. A first step towards guaranteeing a minimum income, which does no more than attempt to plug a gap in the existing system, would thus be to extend entitlement to family credit to all full-time workers.

The effects of such a scheme have been analysed using the new IFS tax and benefit model, TAXBEN 2. This microcomputer simulation model contains a comprehensive description of the UK personal tax and social security system and may be used to examine the effects of specified reform packages. (For details of the structure and operation of the model see Johnson *et al.* 1990). It is assumed here for simplicity that any entitlement to family credit is claimed and thus that the take up rate under the present system and under any reformed system is 100 per cent.

The effects of an extension of family credit on the weekly net incomes of different groups of the population is shown in Table 4.1, and is illustrated diagrammatically in Figure 4.1.

TABLE 4.1 EFFECTS OF EXTENSION OF FAMILY CREDIT BY FAMILY TYPE

Family type	Average gain (£ per week)	
	Of those affected	Whole group
Single employed	8.00	0.57
Single earner couple	18.60	0.55
Two earner couple	9.76	0.10
POPULATION	9.12	0.19

As we would expect, it is mainly single people and couples where only one partner is working who benefit from such a reform. Among those affected by the change, gains to single employees were the smallest but were relatively widespread among the group. The gains to single earner couples tended to be larger, but were concentrated among a smaller number. These patterns are backed up by the fact that of the 650,000 tax units who benefit from this reform, around 550,000 are single people. The effects of the reform on tax units classified by gross income range are shown in Table 4.2.

TABLE 4.2 EFFECTS OF EXTENSION OF FAMILY CREDIT BY GROSS INCOME RANGE

Gross income range[a] (£ per week)	Average gain (£ per week)
	Whole group
below 10.00	0.03
10.00 – 49.99	0.90
50.00 – 99.99	0.85
100.00 – 149.99	0.05
POPULATION	0.19

[a] The measure of gross income used here is the original income, including earnings and investment income but excluding social security benefits, of the family unit as a whole.

In terms of gross income levels, almost all the gains from the extension of family credit go to those with incomes below £100 per week. There are virtually no gains for those on the lowest incomes since there are no full time employees in this income range. (The small gains shown in Table 4.2 are accruing to a few self employed people with particularly low incomes when their income data was recorded).

I estimate that the total cost of such a reform, on the assumption of full take-up, would be around £350m, or an extra two-thirds of family credit expenditure in 1990–91.

It is important to see, however, that this minor alteration to the structure of family credit does little more than attempt to patch up a benefit which currently reaches only around half of those it is intended to reach. The above analysis has assumed that there is full take-up of entitlement to the extended family credit, but in fact perhaps between one-third and one-half of the newly entitled would probably fail to claim the benefit. In many respects the extension of family credit to childless full-timers does no more to guarantee them an income than does the present system of family credit on the 300,000 plus who, for whatever reason, fail to claim it.

In the light of this problem we turn now to examine a more fundamental reform of the tax and benefit system as it affects full-timers, which moves more substantially in the direction of a guaranteed minimum income for this group.

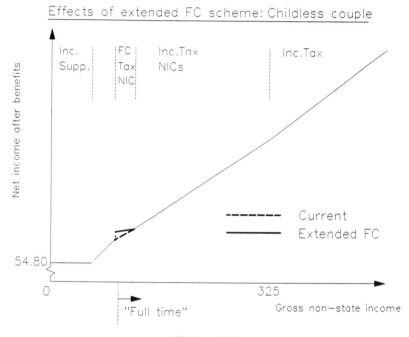

Effects of extended FC scheme: Childless couple

FIGURE 4.1

ii) Family Credit – Income Tax Integration

The present tax and benefit system as it applies to families with children is shown in Figure 4.2. (for ease of exposition I ignore the effects of the Housing Benefit system, although in the detailed simulations full account is taken of the effects of our reforms on that benefit). The reader should note that the shallower the slope the higher the withdrawal rate of benefit (and later of tax) as income rises.

At low levels of income such a family would be entitled to income support. As gross income rises (above a small disregard not shown in the diagram) income support is withdrawn pound for pound so that net income remains unchanged. Once a member of the family unit is working 24 hours a week or more, he is deemed to be working 'full-time' and eligibility for income support ceases.[3] At this point the family becomes entitled to claim

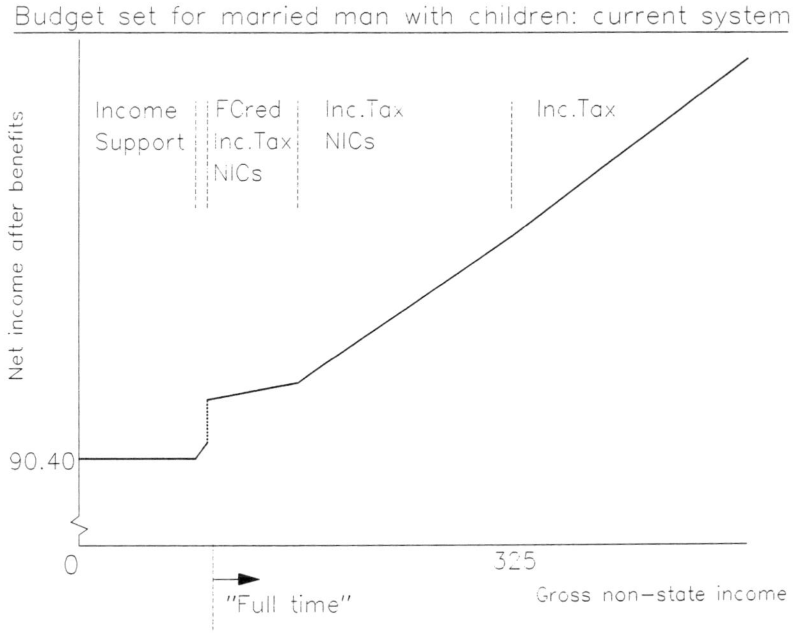

Budget set for married man with children: current system

FIGURE 4.2

family credit. It is also assumed for simplicity that income tax becomes payable at around this point, and that employee NICs continue to be payable.

Family credit has been designed to encourage people to take low paid jobs by making total remuneration when employed greater than income when unemployed. As Figure 4.2 shows, there is a sharp jump in net income as the individual passes the 24 hours per week point, providing a clear financial incentive to take low paid full-time work. Family credit is, however, withdrawn rapidly as income rises, although the particular income level at which the benefit is exhausted will depend upon the age and number of children. Beyond this point, the family receives no income-related benefit and pays a combination of income tax and national insurance. This situation continues until earnings pass the National Insurance ceiling (£325 p.w. in Autumn 1989, now £350) above which no further NICs are payable. Finally then the individual pays only income tax on any extra pound earned, first at the basic rate and ultimately at the higher rate of tax (not shown on the diagram).

As Figure 4.2 suggests, only a relatively small number of families is entitled to family credit, and as has been noted, even among those who are entitled, only around 50 per cent actually take up that entitlement. A further feature of the present system is that those who are receiving the benefit face a very high rate of withdrawal as income rises. The combination of higher income tax and NICs and lower family credit means that an increase of £1 in gross income yields only 20p more in net income.

In the light of these problems I consider now a reform which might be expected to improve take-up of family credit and would also significantly reduce the marginal tax rate faced by full-timers on low wages. The principal cost of this reform, it should be noted at the outset, is an increase in the marginal tax faced by all other full-time workers, as well as losses for those further up the income distribution. The structure of the proposed reform is illustrated in Figure 4.3.

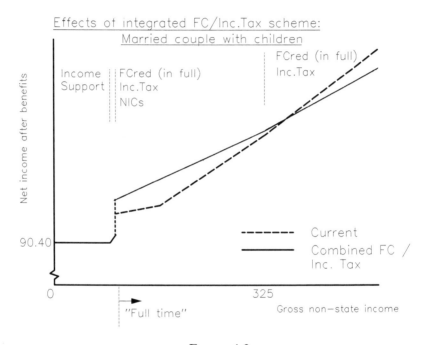

Effects of integrated FC/Inc.Tax scheme:
Married couple with children

FIGURE 4.3

Under the scheme shown in Figure 4.3, all full-time workers would become entitled to family credit, regardless of their income. They would receive the full family credit for a family of their size and composition which would not be withdrawn as income rose. Instead the increased expenditure would be financed by a higher rate of income tax. The scheme might be appropriately characterised as an integration of the family credit and income tax schemes. This is because family credit no longer has its own separate withdrawal mechanism, but rather the net benefit from payments of family credit is progressively reduced via the income tax system. In fact, our simulations suggest that a uniform income tax rate of 44–45 per cent could be used to finance such scheme at no net cost, and this tax rate and structure is reflected in the diagram. It is important to note however that there is no logical reason why a single uniform rate of withdrawal need be applied. Many proposed schemes of this sort would include a more rapid rate of withdrawal at low incomes. (See for example the scheme set out in Dilnot *et al.* 1984).

Table 4.3 shows how families of different types would be affected by this combination of a universal family credit for full-time workers and a significantly higher rate of income tax. (A rate of 44 per cent is used in the simulation, giving the scheme a net cost of £900m. This is significantly less than the cost of reducing the basic rate of income tax by 1p).

TABLE 4.3. EFFECTS OF INTEGRATION OF FAMILY CREDIT AND INCOME TAX BY FAMILY TYPE

Family type	Average gain (whole group) (£ per week)
Single unemployed	−0.20
Single employed	−1.71
Single parent family	4.68
Unemployed couple, no children	−1.25
Unemployed couple with children	−0.98
Single earner couple, no children	2.06
Single earner couple with children	12.51
Two earner couple, no children	−8.18
Two earner couple, with children	13.19
Single Pensioner	−3.97
Couple Pensioner	−0.50
POPULATION	0.59

Table 4.3 shows that it is families with children who do best out of this reform, particularly where either one or both of the parents is at work. This is because a universal family credit is more generous to families with children and so the gains from the payment of full family credit are only fully offset by higher income tax at relatively high incomes for this group. There are two main groups which lose in cash terms from the reform.

The first and most worrying is those who are not in full-time employment (and hence do not benefit from the enhanced family credit) but who have taxable income (and so lose from the sharp increase in the income tax rate). This accounts for the losses among slightly better off pensioners and the unemployed. The other group which loses, and indeed bears the brunt of financing the enhanced family credit, is those on high incomes. As Figure 4.3 suggests, at incomes of around £350 p.w. and above the net benefit from the newly available family credit is exhausted by the higher income tax rate, and these losses increase as income rises. This finding is reflected in Table 4.4 which shows the effect of the reform on families classified by gross income range.

TABLE 4.4. EFFECTS OF INTEGRATION OF FAMILY CREDIT AND INCOME TAX
BY GROSS INCOME RANGE

Gross income range (£ per week)	Average gain (whole group) (£ per week)
below 10.00	0.19
10.00 – 49.99	1.30
50.00 – 99.99	7.08
100.00 – 149.99	8.40
150.00 – 199.99	8.09
200.00 – 249.99	6.62
250.00 – 299.99	4.72
300.00 – 399.99	−2.67
400.00 – 499.99	−14.96
500.00 – 599.99	−28.61
600.00 – 999.99	−43.35
1000.00 and above	−74.95
POPULATION	0.59

Although we have already seen that relatively poor groups such as
pensioners and the unemployed face small losses from the reform, from
Table 4.4 we see that it is in fact high income earners who suffer the major
losses. Those with gross incomes in the £50–£200 p.w. range are on average
net beneficiaries by about £7–£8 p.w.

In assessing a reform such as this we must however examine not only the
gains and losses which it produces for different groups but also the effects of
the reform on the distribution of marginal tax rates. The illustration in
Figure 4.3 suggests that a small group of families will now face lower
marginal rates (those previously in receipt of family credit and now facing a
lower withdrawal rate), but that the majority of full-time workers and other
income tax payers will face a higher marginal rate. The relative magnitude of
these effects is shown in aggregate in Table 4.5.

TABLE 4.5. INTEGRATION OF FAMILY CREDIT AND INCOME TAX:
AGGREGATE EFFECTS ON MARGINAL TAX RATES

Marginal tax rate (%)	Number of individuals (thousands)	
	Current system	Integrated FC / Income tax
Under 20	19,100	19,600
20 – 29	6,200	200
30 – 39	14,800	—
40 – 49	1,000	8,100
50 – 59	—	13,900
60 – 90	1,400	800
100 and over	500	500
POPULATION	43,000	43,000

Table 4.5 illustrates the quite dramatic effects of the reform in question on the structure of marginal tax rates. Under the currrent system about 40 per cent of individuals are either non-taxpayers or pay only NICs and would lose nothing in income-related benefits if they were to experience a small rise in their income. These people have marginal rates of less than 20 per cent and this proportion stays broadly unchanged under the reformed system. Another 45 to 50 per cent of the population, or 21 million individuals, are currently paying tax at the basic rate with 15 million of these paying NICs at the margin as well. This produces a combined marginal tax rate of 25 per cent for those just paying income tax, and a rate of either 32 or 34 per cent for those paying NICs as well.

Under the reform option the single income tax rate is 44 per cent, and so most individuals paying income tax alone face an increase in their marginal rate from 25 per cent to 44 per cent. Those paying NICs as well go from 32/34 per cent to 51/53 per cent overall—in each case a significant increase. We should note that relatively few of those in the 40–49 per cent range move to the 50–59 per cent range. This is because of the way in which we have treated higher rate taxpayers. For simplicity it has been assumed that the 44 per cent income tax rate would apply to all taxpayers, including those currently facing a 40 per cent marginal rate. Consequently, these people (who pay no NICs at the margin because they are over the upper earnings limit) remain in the 40–50 per cent group.

The main improvement comes in relation to the higher rates of withdrawal. Currently the withdrawal of family credit or housing benefit leaves 1.4 million individuals with marginal rates between 60 and 99 per cent. Under the reform the main group to be taken out of this range is those who already received family credit. Most of these, in common with most other full-time workers, now face a marginal rate in the 50 to 60 per cent range.

Aggregate comparisons such as these may, however, somewhat overstate the possible incentive problems attendant upon a reform of this kind. In Table 4.6 we illustrate this by breaking down the changes in marginal tax rates by family type.

TABLE 4.6. INTEGRATION OF FAMILY CREDIT AND INCOME TAX: EFFECTS ON MARGINAL TAX RATES OF SELECTED GROUPS (CURRENT SYSTEM IN BRACKETS) – CELL TOTALS REPRESENT MILLIONS OF INDIVIDUALS

	Range of marginal tax rates					
	0–19	20–29	30–39	40–49	50–59	60+
Single earner couples						
– with children	2.8 (2.5)	0.0 (0.6)	0.0 (1.6)	0.9 (0.1)	1.5 (0.0)	0.2 (0.6)
– without children	1.3 (1.3)	0.0 (0.4)	0.0 (0.9)	0.5 (0.1)	0.8 (0.0)	0.2 (0.2)
Two earner couples						
– with children	1.7 (1.6)	0.0 (1.2)	0.0 (3.6)	1.8 (0.2)	3.2 (0.0)	0.1 (0.3)
– without children	0.7 (0.7)	0.0 (1.3)	0.0 (3.6)	1.8 (0.3)	3.3 (0.0)	0.1 (0.1)
Single employees	0.3 (0.3)	0.0 (0.6)	0.0 (5.0)	0.8 (0.1)	4.8 (0.0)	0.3 (0.3)
Pensioners	7.2 (7.2)	0.1 (1.9)	0.0 (0.1)	2.0 (0.2)	0.0 (0.0)	0.2 (0.1)

A first point to note is that when examining the growth in the numbers facing a marginal rate of 44 per cent rather than 25 per cent almost one-quarter is accounted for by taxpaying pensioners facing a higher tax rate. Thus although an extra 7 million individuals now face marginal rates in the 40–49 per cent range, the effect on work incentives may not be as serious as would appear at first sight since around 2 million of these are pensioners.[4] We also see from Table 4.6 that around 600,000 couples with children no longer face the highest rates of withdrawal but that this has been achieved at a cost of a sharp increase in the numbers of these families facing rates in the 40–59 per cent range. Among childless families there is no gain at higher rates (since none of these families were previously receiving family credit) but there is again an increase in the numbers moving into the 40–59 per cent range.

Nonetheless, these results highlight a fundamental trade-off which must be addressed in considering any reform of this nature. Within the constraint of a given budget, increased generosity to those on lower incomes is possible (as illustrated by Figure 4.3), but only at the cost of higher marginal rates. In the particular example chosen it was decided to spread the effects of this increased marginal rate evenly over the whole working population. It should be noted however that this is not a logically necessary feature of such a reform. As in the present system, it is possible to concentrate still higher marginal rates on the few, in order that the majority should continue to face relatively low marginal rates.

One important attraction of the integrated family credit/income tax scheme set out above is that it might be expected to lead to a significant improvement in the take up of family credit. Since the benefit would be paid to *all* full time workers and not merely a small proportion, then public awareness of the benefit would be heightened. Furthermore, this universality would be likely to reduce significantly any stigma attached to being a recipient of a state benefit.

It should be noted also that there is no reason why the full family credit should not continue to be paid to the mother as at present. Dilnot (1987) has proposed a scheme very similar to the one which is being considered here expressly designed to combine improved take-up of family credit with continued payment to the mother. In the Dilnot scheme the family credit would be paid in the same way as child benefit with no need to claim separately. The principal difference between the Dilnot scheme and the reform option shown in Figure 4.3 is that Dilnot envisages an initial and rapid withdrawal of the net benefits from the family credit via the tax system rather than a single uniform rate of tax across all incomes.

In this section then I have examined the implications of a universal family credit scheme for full-time workers, seeing how it would be likely to improve take-up and move towards a guaranteed minimum income for families with a full-time worker. In the final section I consider how this approach might be extended to apply to the whole population.

iii) Family Credit—Income Support—Income Tax Integration

When considering ways in which the present social security system fails to guarantee a minimum income to families three main exceptions were discussed: non-coverage, non-take-up and disqualifications. The first of these, non-coverage related mainly to childless working families and might be dealt with by a more extensive family credit scheme with restructuring to improve take-up. One such scheme has been set out in section ii) above. Non-take-up has also been a problem relating particularly to those in work, but even among those entitled to Income Support, only around 80 per cent of families are believed to claim their entitlement. Thus a reform which would also reduce obstacles to take-up of Income Support such as ignorance, stigma, and costs of claiming would help to plug another gap in the present system. If such a reform furthermore covered those presently excluded on the grounds of the various disqualifications such as non-availability for work/excessive levels of capital etc., then the resulting system would come close to guaranteeing a minimum income at least at a family level.

One such system, which is based on the same principles as that proposed above for full-time workers is illustrated in Figure 4.4 for the example of a family with children.

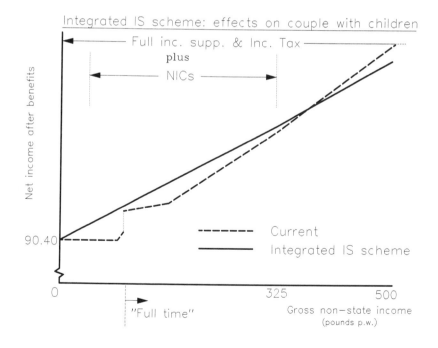

FIGURE 4.4

The way the proposed system would work would be for the state to pay a specified amount of benefit to *all* families which would not depend on income. If fully taken up, this would guarantee a minimum level of income to all families. This payment would not itself be withdrawn as income rises but all other income would become taxable (above a small allowance to avoid the administrative cost of collecting large numbers of tiny amounts of tax). The tax rate would be higher than the current basic rate (probably needing to be around 40 per cent), because the income tax system would now be doing the job of the old income support taper in recouping the net benefit from the social security as income rose. Since all families would be entitled to a full payment bringing them to income support levels, there would of course be no need for a separate family credit system. The new structure would thus amalgamate Income Support, Family Credit and income tax into a single system where all families receive a payment related to family composition, and then all other income above a small allowance is taxed at a single rate.

The impact of a complete integration of IS, FC and income tax in the manner described on the net incomes of different family types is shown in Table 4.7.

TABLE 4.7. EFFECTS OF INTEGRATION OF FAMILY CREDIT, INCOME SUPPORT AND INCOME TAX BY FAMILY TYPE

Family type	Average gain (whole group) (£ per week)
Single unemployed	0.30
Single employed	−1.90
Single parent family	4.97
Unemployed couple, no children	5.22
Unemployed couple with children	2.35
Single earner couple, no children	7.32
Single earner couple with children	17.61
Two earner couple, no children	−18.61
Two earner couple with children	6.25
Single Pensioner	0.28
Couple Pensioner	0.17
POPULATION	0.62

We see from Table 4.7 that the main losers from this reform are again childless families and particularly childless couples where both parners are earning. For a given level of income, couples with two earners do less well because they are most affected by the effective abolition of all tax allowances. Just as with the universal family credit scheme considered earlier, this reform also tends to favour those with children because the initial payment of income support is larger for such families, and with a lower rate of withdrawal net losses only occur at higher incomes. This may be seen clearly by examining Figure 4.5 which also shows the effect of this reform but this time on a childless married couple.

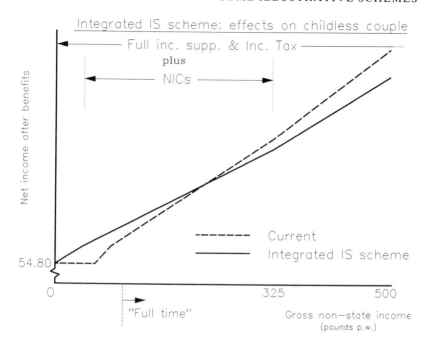

FIGURE 4.5

Figures 4.4 and 4.5 are on the same scale and show clearly that losses occur for childless couples at much lower incomes, because the net benefit of their (smaller) income support payment is more quickly tapered away. The effect of the reform broken down by gross income range is shown for all families in Table 4.8.

TABLE 4.8. EFFECTS OF INTEGRATION OF FAMILY CREDIT, INCOME SUPPORT AND INCOME TAX BY GROSS INCOME RANGE

Gross income range (£ per week)	Average gain (whole group) (£ per week)
below 10.00	1.67
10.00 – 49.99	5.78
50.00 – 99.99	6.85
100.00 – 149.99	6.57
150.00 – 199.99	6.79
200.00 – 249.99	5.50
250.00 – 299.99	2.78
300.00 – 399.99	−6.64
400.00 – 499.99	−18.62
500.00 – 599.99	−30.13
600.00 – 999.99	−35.39
1000.00 and above	−32.21
POPULATION	0.62

Those with the lowest gross incomes are on average only small gainers from the reform. This is because many are already receiving an income close to the full income support level and thus have relatively little scope for gains. In the case of pensioners a simple IS/FC/Income tax integration scheme would in fact lead to small losses on average because of the higher tax rate being applied to unearned income such as occupational pensions and investment income. This would on average outweigh the gain from a comprehensive entitlement to full income support. In order to prevent such losses however the particular scheme under examination here contains a small addition to the pensioner premiums available under income support which have been set to prevent pensioners as a whole from losing from this reform.

As with the FC/income tax integration scheme, gains rise with income up to around £200 p.w. and then decline sharply with net losses beginning for those with gross incomes in excess of £300. It is however interesting to note that the very richest families lose rather less under this scheme. This is because the overall rate of tax required for a broadly revenue neutral scheme is rather lower at around 40 per cent (compared with 44 per cent for the FC/income tax scheme).

The effects of this complete integration option on marginal tax rates are analogous to those for the FC/income tax integration scheme as Table 4.9 shows.

TABLE 4.9. INTEGRATION OF FAMILY CREDIT, INCOME SUPPORT AND INCOME TAX: AGGREGATE EFFECTS ON MARGINAL TAX RATES

| Marginal tax rate (%) | Number of individuals (thousands) | |
	Current system	Integrated FC / IS/Income tax
under 20	19,100	14,400
20 – 29	6,200	200
30 – 39	14,800	5,400
40 – 49	1,000	20,500
50 – 59	—	1,100
60 – 99	1,400	1,200
100 and over	500	100
POPULATION	43,000	43,000

A first feature of the change is that the numbers with very low marginal rates (below 20 per cent) falls by about one-quarter compared with the present system. This result arises from the effective abolition of all but a token tax allowance. The precise numbers affected in this way would, however, tend to be highly sensitive to the precise level of residual allowance chosen. In the current simulation the single allowance is set at £10 per week (compared with £57 per week at present) and this inevitably creates a large increase in the number of families paying relatively small amounts of tax.

From Table 4.9 we see that the cost of removing around 600,000 people from rates in excess of 60 per cent by means of a single withdrawal rate is that almost half the adult population becomes faced with marginal rates between 40 and 50 per cent. It should be stressed that this dramatic change is primarily a consequence of the single withdrawal rate rather than of the introduction of an income guarantee as such. Alternative income guarantee schemes could be designed where the burden of high marginal tax rates was more sharply focused. The effects of the reform on marginal rates subdivided by family type are shown in Table 4.10.

TABLE 4.10. INTEGRATION OF FAMILY CREDIT, INCOME SUPPORT AND INCOME TAX: EFFECTS ON MARGINAL TAX RATES OF SELECTED GROUPS (CURRENT SYSTEM IN BRACKETS)—CELL TOTALS REPRESENT MILLIONS OF INDIVIDUALS.

	Range of marginal tax rates					
	0–19	20–29	30–39	40–49	50–59	60+
Single earner couples						
– with children	2.3 (2.5)	0.1 (0.6)	0.6 (1.6)	1.7 (0.1)	0.3 (0.0)	0.4 (0.6)
– without children	0.9 (1.3)	0.0 (0.4)	0.4 (0.9)	1.0 (0.1)	0.2 (0.0)	0.3 (0.2)
Two earner couples						
– with children	0.2 (1.6)	0.0 (1.2)	1.3 (3.6)	4.8 (0.2)	0.3 (0.0)	0.3 (0.3)
– without children	0.0 (0.7)	0.0 (1.3)	0.8 (3.6)	4.8 (0.3)	0.1 (0.0)	0.1 (0.1)
Single employees	0.2 (0.3)	0.0 (0.6)	0.4 (5.0)	5.4 (0.1)	0.1 (0.0)	0.3 (0.3)
Pensioners	5.5 (7.2)	0.0 (1.9)	1.6 (0.1)	2.2 (0.2)	0.1 (0.0)	0.1 (0.1)

The most worrying additional information contained in Table 4.10 relates to the marginal rates now faced by two earner couples. We see a fall of 2 million in the numbers of individuals in two earner couples facing very low marginal rates. This group is dominated by married women earning amounts below the existing personal allowance. Under the reformed scheme such individuals begin to pay tax at very low incomes and may thus be discouraged from retaining their job. Similarly, their employers might be reluctant to bear the administrative costs if such workers were brought into the PAYE system. Such effects are not included in our assessment of the overall costs of the various schemes under consideration, but would clearly need to be borne in mind.

The main attraction of this final reform option is that it comes very close to guaranteeing a minimum income to all families at a broadly acceptable level. If income support, family credit and the income tax mechanism were all consolidated into a single system applicable to all then take-up problems would largely disappear. All groups would be covered by the scheme and there would be no disqualifications on the grounds of non-availability for work etc. Such a scheme could legitimately claim many of the advantages set out earlier in this chapter.

Conclusions

Under the present UK social security system large numbers of families fail to achieve a level of income equal to the income support/supplementary benefit line. I have argued that this situation will not be significantly improved by minor alterations to the existing system and that a more fundamental reform of the tax and benefit system would be necessary. A system which genuinely guaranteed a minimum income to all families would have a number of attractions, but might face difficulties in the area of incentive effects, political acceptability and cost. In the light of this analysis I have examined a series of reforms including a full-blown family-based income guarantee scheme. This latter scheme provided a guaranteed minimum income for all families at the present income support level, but was financed by a uniform marginal income tax rate of 40 per cent. It is my hope that the analysis presented in this paper will prompt further discussion of income guarantee schemes by highlighting their attractions and also the costs which they would impose.

NOTES

1 For a discussion of the causes of non-take-up of supplementary benefit see Fry and Stark (1987).
2 As income after tax and NICs increases by £1, income support is reduced by £1, or family credit by 70p.
3 The precise income level at which 'full-time work' begins will of course depend upon the prevailing wage rate. In the diagram it is assumed that at around 22 hours work the family has just begun to earn enough for their net income plus Child Benefit to exceed the income support line.
4 We might however be concerned about more long term disincentives to save among those nearing retirement age.

5 Concluding Thoughts

Samuel Brittan

Cost, Affordability and Compromise

A Basic Income Guarantee large enough to provide everyone in or out of work with at least a conventional subsistence income, which would be withdrawn only at the normal tax rate, would be prohibitively expensive at present. Mrs Parker investigates the costs of providing a Basic Income, which aims to pay each adult some 30 per cent of average pre-tax earnings, using as a basis somewhere between average earnings for men and women and average earnings for men alone. (This would give a target of roughly £80 per week for 1989–90 pay levels). She estimates that to provide this sum an Income Tax rate (incorporating National Insurance) of 68 to 86 per cent would be required. The lower percentage assumes the abolition of all reliefs for mortgage interest and private pension contributions.

Steven Webb outlines in his final scheme in Chapter 4 a proposal to integrate Family Credit, Income Support and Income Tax with a uniform withdrawal and tax rate. He has managed to reduce the cost, compared with other schemes, by using a household as distinct from individual basis of assessment, and his target minimum income is lower. Even so the revenue cost on a 'no loser' basis is £30 billion per annum. If the resources have to be recovered from Income Tax, a rise in the Income Tax rate from 25 to 40 per cent would be required, or 49 per cent when employee National Insurance contributions are added.

When indirect taxes, employers' contributions, the Community Charge, business and other taxes are all added in, the total burden is heavy. On a modest estimate the typical family would face a gross tax bill of more than 70 per cent of original income. Even if we could persuade people to look at their net tax burden after offsetting the Basic Income payment, the resulting burden would still be high enough to encounter formidable resistance. Unless and until a robotic revolution which makes the whole community several times richer at an acceptable environmental price really does arrive, there is no alternative but to think of a gradual move towards Basic Incomes with many compromises and transitional phases.

There are two kinds of compromise. The Basic Income can be a modest sum (what Meade calls an Inadequate Social Dividend) relying on conditional

45

benefits to achieve the minimum. Alternatively, reformers can go for a subsistence Basic Minimum at an early stage, but retain a withdrawal rate, higher than the Income Tax rate, for those receiving benefit. Thus some elements of the poverty trap would be retained which one would hope to reduce with the growth of the national wealth.

Mrs Parker's compromise is to start with a very modest Basic Income. This is also the approach of the Liberal Democrat 1989 Green Paper which advocates for its 'second stage' reforms a Citizen's Income of £10.30 per week. The two compromises are not mutually exclusive. It is possible to combine a modest Basic Income payment with a withdrawal rate above the income tax rate, while still making an improvement on the present state of affairs.

The point to remember is that some gain would remain, even if Basic Income were inadequate to provide an acceptable social minimum and still had to be topped up with some conditional benefits, or if there were, over a range of income, an effective withdrawal rate greater than the basic rate of income tax. The best must not be the enemy of the good.

Basic Elements

If we are to have a systematic discussion, rather than a confusing battle between each reformer's favourite scheme, it will help to unpack the Basic Income ideas into its components. Here is a list, not necessarily comprehensive.

1. *Speed and Automaticity*: The paradigm case is Child Benefit. This is payable across the counter at Post Offices speedily and without complication, and take-up is nearly 100 per cent.

2 *Integration*: Tax and benefit are set off against each other, so that each affected citizen either makes a payment or receives benefit with no 'churning' (that is there are no tax payments offset by benefit receipts).

3. *Symmetry*: The rights, conditions and obligations of those who are net receipients of benefit are a mirror image of those who are net payers of tax.

4. *Unconditionality*:
(a) Of status. The benefit is paid without questions about incapacity, attempts to find work and so on.
(b) Of means. The benefit is paid of right without any questions about capital and other means.

5. *Adequacy*: The payment should provide a genuine subsistence minimum. The concept is inescapably subjective and conventional. It acquires meaning when we realise that many existing benefits do not even *aim* to provide such a minimum. (Generosity is represented by the size of the basic payment or tax credit OA in Fig 1.1 of Chapter 1).

6. *Uniform Withdrawal Rate*: Benefit is withdrawn at no more than the normal tax rate (including both present Income Tax and employee National Insurance contributions). Apart from being desirable in itself this characteristic, were it attainable, would make it easier to merge the tax and social security systems.

Until a country can both afford and has the administrative set-up for a fully fledged Basic Income a choice has to be made along some of the above dimensions. I believed for a long time that the administrative aspects were secondary and that the key feature of a Basic Income scheme could be achieved by modifying the rates and conditions of existing tax and social security schemes. But the low take-up of income-releated benefits has convinced me that a reform of the machinery is also required.

There are conflicting objectives even among administrative reforms. On the one hand, full tax and social security integration will make the system more transparent; and by setting-off social security receipts against income tax it might persuade more taxpayers to accept the burden of a Basic Income scheme. On the other hand, the aspect most desired by recipients is speed and automaticity as achieved by the over-the-counter principle of Child Benefit. Over-the-counter payment (which covers also direct payment into a bank account) has proved to be the best method of securing high take-up from low income families and ensuring that payments are made speedily when they are most required.

There are genuine problems in integrating two bodies—the Department of Social Security and the Inland Revenue—with very different procedures, traditions and types of client. For instance the adjustment of Income Tax liabilities to changing circumstances takes several months. Unless and until the tax and Social Security systems have not only been fully merged but are able to make adjustments within weeks, benefit recipients will probably prefer to accept some 'churning', for the sake of receiving their payment *across the counter*, like Child Benefit today.

A good compromise would be to let the household choose for itself whether to accept an integrated payment to or from the Revenue, or whether to receive benefits directly on the over-the-counter principle. (The mother should always have the option of asking for the latter.)

The third desirable quality is symmetry. The integration of the Department of Social Security with the Inland Revenue will help achieve it. But it is partly a matter of implicit tax rates through the income spectrum.

The cost of unconditionality of status would depend on behavioural reaction; above all on how many people ceased actively to look for work, or decided to work fewer hours, once scrutiny came to an end. My own hunch is that the overwhelming majority of working age single adults and heads of households would prefer to have jobs rather than subsist in idleness on what would be a very exiguous basic minimum. The present cost of both Unemployment Benefit and Income Support for the unemployed is much less than in popular imagination and a fraction of the cost of state pensions.

Adequacy is a matter of the size of the transfer the taxpaying majority of the population is prepared to make to the less well off minority. Prevailing judgements are reflected in the Income Support scales (together with Housing Benefit) reported in Chapter 3. Adequacy is then a matter of filling the gaps due to low take-up, non-availability of Family Credit to families without children and other lacunae. Further gaps arise from conditionality, e.g. the withholding of benefit from people who have left jobs. The Thatcher Government has also widened the difference between Income Support for working age recipients and pensioners, and between under and over-25s. These are deliberate acts to discourage people from living on benefit and would have to be reconsidered under a Basic Income approach.

Overwhelmingly the most expensive aspect of Basic Income schemes is the sixth one, namely a withdrawal rate for Basic Incomes no higher than the marginal income tax rate paid by taxpayers. By comparision the cost of eliminating gaps in the safety net is modest. As Steven Webb reports in Chapter 4, the very high cost of his final Basic Income simulation arises, not from unconditionality or plugging gaps, but from saving 600,000 people from having to suffer high withdrawal rates on existing benefit. *I would therefore put Requirement 6, the uniform tax and benefit withdrawal rate, on the back burner.* By this I do not mean indifference to poverty trap effects. Some reduction, for instance, of the 100 per cent withdrawal rate now applying to Income Support would be very welcome. But implicit marginal tax rates will have to be higher for the lowest income households unless and until the Robotic Utopia really arrives. Moreover, if there is a choice between an improvement in the basic minimum (Aspect 5) and moving nearer to a uniform withdrawal rate (Aspect 6), the former may be more important. The aesthetic symmetry of a perfect Basic Income scheme may for a while have to give way to improved adequacy of an imperfect one.

Medium Term Goal

Thus my medium term aim would be something on the lines of Steven Webb's last scheme in Chapter 4 (pages 39 to 43) for integrating Family Credit, Income Support and Income Tax to provide an unconditional basic minimum for all householders. The option of receiving payments from the state across the counter (as with present Child Benefit) for those who preferred that to integration would be retained. The payment would be unconditional depending only on the number of people in the household and ages of the children. 'Means testing' would be achieved through a withdrawal mechanism operated via the tax system, thus achieving a formal symmetry for net beneficiaries and recipients. But there would be one important difference, which would very much lower the 'cost'. This is that the withdrawal rate would continue to be very much higher than the basic rate of income tax, although below the present 100 per cent for Income Support.

Eventually the Income Guarantee would remove the need for contributory National Insurance benefits, of which by far and away the most important is the basic state pension. Neither author has, however, attempted to tackle this hornets' nest. Most people believe, however wrongly, that they have paid for state pensions and similar benefits; and any phasing out would have to lie many years ahead. Moreover, so long as the withdrawal rate of the Basic Income remained very high, the cost savings would not be overwhelming. The future of the residual state earnings related pension scheme would also come into question. But here again, we have not attempted to take a view.

An Incremental Approach

It is important to keep in mind the capital endowment idea. Unfortunately, two opportunities to hand over endowments to all citizens were lost, when UK state oil revenues were merged with other revenues in the 1970s, and when it was decided to sell privatised stock to investors in the 1980s without earmarking even a proportion to be handed over as citizen stock. The best opportunities in this direction are now to be found in Eastern Europe where state owned enterprises are being denationalised and where there is no investing public with the means to purchase the privatised stock. In Britain we can still be alert for citizen ownership opportunities when they ocur. But regrettably the main thrust towards Basic Incomes will have to come for the time being from the social security side.

Basic Incomes are an approach to income support and should not be a messianic movement. One result of unpacking the idea into its component parts at the beginning of this chapter has been to show that it does not have to be all-or-nothing. A start can be made with reforming the existing system, well before even the limited integration proposal just discussed becomes possible.

One place to start reforming the existing system would be to end the complete cutoff of both Income Support and Unemployment Benefit when a job is taken. For reasons of cost and incentive the taper might have to be very steep. But it should be possible to allow people who take low paid or part-time jobs some residual benefit. This would end the unemployment trap, by which single persons and married ones without children can in principle be better off on benefit than at work. Families with children are in principle catered for by Family Credit; and part of the same reform would be to make benefit levels for Family Credit consistent with those for Income Support.

A different reform for older people would be to provide all people of pension age with the same benefit scales, irrespective of whether what they are drawing is called Income Support or state pension. If that were done, the time would be ripe for re-examining the myth of National Insurance and for either transforming contributions into a payroll level or amalgamating them with Income Tax.

A simpler but more controversial change would be to raise the level of Income Support to people of working age to the pensioner level and to eliminate or reduce the discrimination against the single person under 25.

Child Benefit and Family Credit

The most interesting direction of change, however, would be to build on two existing benefits which do contain elements of Basic Income—Child Benefit and Family Credit. Child Benefits are embryonic Basic Incomes in being paid without conditions for every 'caring parent' (normally the mother) at £7.25 per child irrespective of other income. Take-up is almost 100 per cent. But Child Benefit is not meant to be enough to bring up the children covered, even on the most rudimentary minimum, let alone the rest of the family.

Family Credit has more of the characteristics normally associated with Negative Income Tax. It is an innovation, dating back in its earliest form to Keith Joseph in 1971 (when it was called Family Income Supplement), designed to top up the incomes of families on low earnings, and thus to encourage the breadwinner to choose work rather than the dole. It is withdrawn at a rate of 70 per cent as income rises.

The two benefits have very different supporters. Family Credit attracts Radical Right partisans of selectivity and Child Benefit *bien pensant* and centre-left partisans of universality. The virtues and defects are mirror images of each other. Family Credit is in principle more generous and concentrates available resources on where they are needed—if only people would claim them. Child Benefit is paid across the counter without demeaning inquiries into other means. As recipients have to pay only normal Income Tax and National Insurance contributions, there is no specially high withdrawal rate and there are no poverty trap effects as income rises.

Because of its universality, Child Benefit is expensive, involving an annual cost of £4bn. in 1990–91 to provide the modest sum of £7.25 per child, a level at which it was frozen in 1987. Family Credit, with an annual cost of around 0.5bn, provided, on the other hand, a weekly supplement averaging £25 to 320,000 recipients. Unfortunately, Family Credit is plagued by the problems of low take-up; as already discussed one-third of the available budget is unclaimed and one-half of potential recipients do not apply. There is also an average interval of 23 working days between a claim for Family Credit and the initial payout. The amount payable is fixed for six months, even if family circumstances deteriorate. Thus the benefit is not a secure lifeline for the part-time, casual or seasonal worker.

The relative claims of the two benefits are always topical because of the perennial campaign to raise Child Benefit or at least restore it to its real level of 1979 (from which it had fallen by 20 per cent in 1989). The proponents of selectivity regard this as very wasteful, because of the spillover of Child Benefit to the family of the Duke of Westminster and other more modestly placed middle income earners, who in no sense need them.

In a recent publication (P Johnson *et al.* 1989), the Institute for Fiscal Studies analysed the consequences of alternative measures on the assumption that the Government has an additional £1bn. per annum available to help families. The IFS writers point out that a crude increase in Child Benefit would be irrelevant to low-income families if all selective benefits were claimed. The reason for this is that any increase in Child Benefit automatically reduces the child addition both to Family Credit and to Income Support by a corresponding amount. Even on realistic take-up assumption, the IFS simulations show that overwhelmingly the largest beneficiaries from an increase in Child and One-Parent Benefit would be family units in the middle and upper ranges. Those with net disposable incomes below £160 per week would gain very little.

The IFS has, however, produced a scheme which combines the across-the-counter advantages of Child Benefit with the greater selectivity desired by the Radical Right. This would involve a large increase in Child Benefit to £34.80 per week, which would continue to be paid to the caring parent. But it would count as taxable income of the father, if his earnings were adequate; and it would, moreover, be withdrawn via the Income Tax mechanism at a specially high marginal rate until it was exhausted.

This package has by far the largest redistributive effect. The greatest gains go to families with relatively low disposable incomes of £100 to £200 per week. The IFS scheme imposes losses on families with gross earnings above £400 per week, which I would not expect the Thatcher Government, or any likely successor, to countenance. The losses arise because the whole of the Child Benefit is eventually taxed away. These losses could be reduced or eliminated if only the *addition* to the Benefit were withdrawn in this way. In that case a Government with £1bn. to spare would still be able to more than double Child Benefit to £15 per week or more.

The IFS proposal for an increase in Child Benefit withdrawable through the tax system contains nearly all the desirable features of Basic Income previously listed: speed, automaticity, symmetry and generosity. It is also a move towards integration, because of the use of the tax system rather than social security means testing, for the withdrawal mechanism. The one goal, which it does not advance is a uniform tax and benefit withdrawal rate.

For the IFS scheme does indeed have the disadvantage of introducing high marginal tax rates towards the bottom of the income distribution. But this is a sacrifice already accepted for the sake of affordability in other schemes, including Family Credit. Indeed a very similar tax withdrawal mechanism already exists in the Age Allowance which is clawed back at a steep rate for pensioners with high incomes. The withdrawable Child Benefit has the advantage of avoiding the indignity of means tested applications and retains the over-the-counter principle.

Tax Credits

The proposed withdrawable increase in Child Benefit would do away with the need for Family Credit. This would leave the problem of low income families without children. An important step forward could be made here by transforming a fraction of the personal tax allowances (£3,000 p.a. for a single person) into a tax credit to be offset against tax bills and paid out as a benefit to those with insufficient tax liabilities. The introduction of tax credits would in a sense be retracing history. For a tax credit scheme was devised by Lord Cockfield for the Heath Government in 1972. The Cockfield scheme was confined to employees, largely for administrative reasons. But this need not be an essential feature today.

Once tax credits and withdrawal Child Benefit were in place the machinery would be there for a Basic Income scheme whereby a household paid tax or received benefit according to means, but without the indignity of DSS means-testing. It would then be but a further incremental slip to integrate Child Benefit and tax credits with Income Support to reach the medium term goal already described.

How Not to Do It

there is an infinite number of proposals *en route* to Basic Incomes; and there is no reason why all Basic Incomes advocates should have the same order of priority for the transition. But that does not mean *carte blanche* approval of all possible changes. I shall illustrate this point by examining proposals—the first from the Conservative and the second from the Labour stable—which run contrary to the spirit of Basic Income and are undesirable in their own right.

The first is that of bringing back Child Tax Allowances. These are deductions from taxable income of so much per child over and above the existing personal allowances. These were abolished in 1979 with bipartisan support precisely because they were worth nothing to those who paid no tax, and little to those who paid low tax. The reintroduction of Child Tax Allowances would take us further away from all the goals mentioned. Assuming that Child Benefit continued (as it would have to in order to avoid a massively regressive effect), it would take us away from both integration and symmetry. The typical family would receive both Child Benefit and the Tax Allowance, while the low income family would receive Child Benefit only (unless it qualified for a means-tested benefit as well). Hardly any families would be taken out of the poverty trap. Speed and automaticity would be slightly less than with Child Benefit. If the Child Allowances were available against the Higher Tax rate, the gain would be predominantly skewed in favour of the better off (P Johnson, *et al.*).

Labour's key proposals also fail any reasonable test. The centrepiece is an increase in the basic pension of at least £5 to £8 per week, to be followed by annual rerating on the faster of prices or earnings growth. As the pension is related both to age and National Insurance contributions, the change would amount to a reinforcement of the conditionality principle. As the cost of the change could well exhaust the resources available, there would probably not be an equivalent rise in the other categories of benefit such as Income

Support. So we would be even further removed from a system of uniform payments, dependent only on family size or special needs.

Each of the last two Labour Governments started off with an across-the-board pensions increase which they spent the remainder of the parliament paying for, and were extremely strapped for cash for other kinds of redistribution—both towards low-income families and towards the poorest minority among the old. Across-the-board increases in state pensions are a wasteful and an inefficient means of helping the poor or relieving poverty; and while politicians may need to buy votes, the rest of us should resist emotional blackmail.

Assessment

Basic incomes are not a costless option and their full realisation is many years ahead. Nor can they solve all social and economic problems. They will not deal with the environment, Third World problems, inflation or training and management in the UK. They are not even a cure-all for poverty, which has deep-seated roots which cannot all be tackled by any feasible changes in financial support. The Basic Income concept may nevertheless represent a way of rectifying some serious holes in the Welfare State safety net and also of gradually improving the incentive structure at the lower end of the income distribution.

The most controversial aspect is the provision of a modest income for all unrelated to work or any other conditions. Yet this may turn out an important advantage in a society where technological change is leading to a widening of pay differentials in the market place and perhaps a rise in the return to capital relative to the rewards of labour. The rudiments of a Basic Income can and should be introduced in an evolutionary and incremental way with plenty of time to stop, look and listen *en route*.

Appendix 1
The Choice of Assessment Unit

Steven Webb

The simulations contained in Chapter 4 have examined income guarantee schemes which use the family as the unit of assessment. This is in keeping with the basis of social security policy over the last 40 years and more. The unit of assessment for income tax until last year was also the family, although the system is now a hybrid between individual and joint taxation of husband and wife. It has however been argued that it would be better to base any income guarantee scheme on the individual rather than on the family. This has in particular been the viewpoint of the Basic Income Research Group (see for example Parker 1989). In this appendix I examine the main issues which will determine the most appropriate choice of assessment unit and explain why disagreement has arisen.

Issues In The Selection Of An Assessment Unit

i) Implications for poverty alleviation.

If there was any question that income sharing was less than complete between husbands and wives, then only an individually assessed income maintenance benefit could hope to completely relieve poverty. Such an ideal may not, however, be possible simply on the grounds of cost. To make such a benefit available at an adequate level to all individuals would involve a major increase in expenditure financed either by sharply increased tax rates, reduced public spending or higher borrowing. It has been calculated that to finance a full 'basic income' type payment (equal to one-third of average earnings) as a replacement for existing cash benefits would require a single tax rate in the 70 to 85 per cent range (Parker 1988). It is of course true that a benefit set at such a level might be in excess of that which was required for 'subsistence' in a modern economy, but it remains the case that cost is the single largest objection to an individually assessed benefit system.

Part of the reason why an individual based scheme might however be unnecessarily expensive is that state payments might simply be 'crowding out' intra-family transactions which would in any case occur. Without detailed information on patterns of income sharing within the family, it is difficult to say whether the extra expenditure necessary for an individual-

54

based scheme would be going to many genuinely needy people. Indeed, such a scheme might be counter-productive in making the guaranteed minimum far lower than would be available under a family based scheme.

ii)   Possible disincentives/distortions arising from choice of base.

In choosing a unit of assessment for social security purposes a second aim must be to minimise the distortions which arise from that choice. Such distortions may take many forms. Labour supply decisions may be affected, the pattern of household formation may be altered, the arrangement of personal financial assets may be changed, all as direct consequences of the choice of assessment unit.

One rather well-documented instance of the implications of a family unit based system of assessment concerns the labour supply behaviour of married women. It has been shown that women married to unemployed men are far less likely to participate in the labour market than the wives of employed husbands, even holding constant other explanatory factors such as numbers of children, region, level of education and so forth.[1] The explanation given for this phenomenon is intimately related to the family unit basis of the benefit system.

When a married man becomes unemployed he will typically be entitled to either Unemployment Benefit or Income Support (or both). Where the husband is receiving unemployment benefit he may receive an addition to his benefit in respect of his wife as long as she is not earning more than the amount of the addition. As soon as she earns a penny more than this amount, the whole addition is wthdrawn. This rather rough-and-ready notion of dpendency means that it makes little sense for the wife to earn any amount in a range of incomes above this cut-off point.

It is not just the notion of dependency inherent in the National Insurance benefit system which gives rise to such problems however. If the husband is receiving income support then even more problems of this nature may arise. If the wife earns more than a small disregarded amount (currently just £5 per week) then every pound she takes home results in a reduction of one pound in her husband's benefit until it is completely exhausted. Once again, the labour supply decisions of the wife are strongly affected by the benefit position of her husband. It becomes the case that a wide range of (possibly attractive) employment opportunities become economically unviable, largely because the basis of assessment of the social security system is the family unit.

It would be fair to note, however, that an individually based system, although free from the sorts of interactions described above, might also have adverse labour supply effects though in a rather different and more indirect way. In this case the problem arises from the way in which a (necessarily) more expensive individually based scheme might be financed. One way which has been proposed would involve the virtual abolition of all income tax allowances.[2] Such a change could not be introduced without itself having considerable labour supply effects. One likely effect would be to discourage participation among secondary earners. Such people, traditionally the group with the most responsive labour supply behaviour, would begin to pay tax on the first pound that they earned, rather than enjoying a tax free allowance of around £57 per week as at present. This would clearly make a range of part time jobs currently held by such workers far less attractive financially.

Although it is clear then that the present family unit basis of assessment has given rise to considerable labour supply distortions, it is by no means certain that an individual based scheme, requiring finance through lower tax allowances or higher tax rates, would fare any better.

Apart from purely economic decisions however, it is also possible that the pattern of household formation could itself be affected by the structure of the benefit system. One attraction of an individual basis of assessment is that it is neutral with respect to marriage. The present system, based on a (narrow) family unit, gives greater weight to two single people than to a married couple and so generates a financial disincentive to marriage.[3] The trend in recent years has been to remove some such features from the tax system,[4] but joint assessment for benefit purposes works against these changes.

iii) Informational requirements

A third criterion by which any proposed unit of assessment should be evaluated is the information requirements which it imposes on claimants and administrators. As well as being an important issue in its own right, this consideration will have an impact on other objectives. Thus the amount of information which has to be gathered will affect the overall cost of the scheme (and hence its potential for poverty alleviation). Similarly a scheme where claimants have to provide a great deal of documentary evidence of incomes etc. may produce lower take-up and again limit the effectiveness of even the most well-structured system of income maintenance.

Furthermore, where initial assessment of entitlement is an administratively complex process there will be an incentive for awards of benefit to be made for longer periods than would otherwise be necessary, and in this way it becomes increasingly likely that benefit will continue to be paid to those who are no longer in need. An example of this is the old Family Income supplement where awards were made for one for year, and were not varied in respect of changing circumstances during the year. Had the process of claiming and assessment been a simpler one, then there would have been no need for such an unresponsive structure of payment.[5] With such considerations in mind I now examine the competing claims of the alternative assessment units.

One of the most complex areas of the present benefit system, arising from the family unit basis of assessment, is determining whether an unmarried claimant who is part of a 'couple' should be treated as married. With continued increases in both the divorce rate and in the proportion of children born outside marriage this issue is likely to remain an important one. Currently factors to be taken into account include whether the relationship is 'stable', what financial arrangements exist between the couple, and (if the claimant wishes to volunteer the information) whether there is any sexual relationship. Such a process raises issues of privacy as well as of administrative cost and complexity, and may of itself deter some individuals from claiming at all. A system of assessment based on a unit wider than the individual must however either contain rules of this sort, or be prepared to accept what on its own terms would be claims from those not genuinely entitled.

A second issue regarding information costs which affects income-related benefits is the need to provide documentary evidence of income information for the specified unit. Clearly, the more narrowly drawn the income unit, the easier it is to assemble and verify the income data which is provided. One consequence of this is that there would then be more incentive to design a system where the amount of benefit paid would respond more flexibly to changes in personal circumstances. In the case of a family unit, collection and verification of income data could be complex and might additionally lessen the financial privacy of other members of the family.

Perhaps the only area where informational considerations would work against the selection of a narrowly defined income unit is where defining ownership of income would be a problem. This might particularly be a problem in the case of unearned income, where members of a couple could adjust ownership of investments (for example) so as to minimise income for benefit purposes. The move towards a system of independent taxation has reduced the financial incentives for such behaviour.

iv) Wider objectives of the social security system.

One of the main themes of writers in the 'basic income' tradition is that social security programmes should have wider objectives than merely the alleviation of poverty.[6] Such objectives have included the fostering of a sense of individual dignity and of value in the eyes of society. One merit of a system of assessment based on the individual, it is claimed, is that no one is dependent on 'hand-outs' from other members of the family or household unit. Although income sharing may actually take place under the present system, the fact that one member of the family (often the husband) receives the money and then decides how much to pass on may reduce the dignity of the other person. This will always be a potential problem where employment income is concerned, but, it is argued, where the state is the main provider of the income then it should not reinforce this pattern.

Similar arguments apply to the notion of the impact of the benefit system on a person's status as a citizen of a particular society. Where an individual is entitled to certain state payments in his/her own right, rather than merely as a member of some broader unit, then a feeling of belonging to that society and of sharing in any prosperity enjoyed by the employed population may be enhanced.

Such views would not however sit comfortably with the present emphasis on avoiding the creation of a 'dependency culture'. Here, the argument is that any receipt of state benefits may lead to an undesirable decline in personal motivation and to increased reliance on state support. In this spirit, recent reforms such as the ending of the householder's rate for SB/Income Support and the lower rate of income support/housing benefit for under 25s have had the clear effect of encouraging young people not to leave home until they are financially independent.[7]

The thrust of recent policy in this area has thus been motivated by the wider objective of eliminating this so-called 'dependency culture'. In this context an important distinction is however drawn between dependence on the state and upon other family members, charities etc. Whilst dependence on the state is seen as undesirable, a reliance on other family members is viewed as being acceptable and as part of the natural function of the family. Advocates of this approach would thus argue that assessment for income-related benefits should be based on the incomes of at least the immediate family rather than just the individual.

Conclusions

The approach taken in the simulations contained in this paper has been to make a subsistence level guaranteed income the over-riding objective. In consequence, the schemes examined here have been based on the family unit. In doing so however, I do not seek to disguise the obvious difficulties of operating a family-based system in the 1990s, nor indeed to minimise the attractions of an individually based scheme. It is hoped rather that this analysis will make more explicit the trade-off involved when choosing between a partial individually based scheme and a full family based income guarantee.

NOTES

1 See for example Kell and Wright (1989).
2 See for example Parker (1989), various schemes.
3 For example, the ratio between the income support rates for two single people and that for a married couple is around 6:5.
4 Measures which have been taken recently with this in mind have included the ending of double mortgage tax relief for cohabiting couples, and the restriction of the additional personal allowance to only one parent in a broken marriage.
5 It is interesting to note that awards of the new Family Credit are payable only for six months at a time, although the new benefit is not conspicuously easier to claim or administer.
6 See for example, Walter (1988), Torry (1988).
7 See Dilnot and Webb (1988) for a discussion of the impact of the 'Fowler' reforms on young single people.

Appendix 2   Towards a Liberal Theory of Distribution

Samuel Brittan

A market economy is the least bad known to mankind for providing goods and services and advancing wealth. Not merely is it more successful than command economies, but experience suggests that it is a necessary, although not sufficient condition for the preservation and development of personal and political freedom. In addition it has built-in devices for error correction and the use of dispersed initiative and information, far superior to those available to the most sophisticated computers of central planning apparatus.

These very simple points should not need too much labouring after recent events in Eastern Europe. Nor should one need to remind people that a successful market system will not take care of itself, or emerge of its own accord, but requires a delicate institutional structure: the rule of law, a monetary system, a state apparatus to provide not only for internal and external security, but to supply or finance goods which the market itself is unlikely to provide in adequate amounts. Moreover, market signals can themselves be distorted—for instance when they fail to convey information about environmental costs. Corrective action here can, however, be of a market oriented kind; for example improving the signals by 'pollution taxes' and 'green subsidies', or more fundamentally, by redefinition of property rights so that polluters are legally liable for the damage they cause. Over and above these institutional and policy features, a market system will not work without a minimum of shared values among its participants and some elements of a common culture.

This is not the place to elaborate these conditions and I have had my say elsewhere.[1] Those who are instinctively sceptical of the recent vogue for market economics should persevere with this Appendix. For my main theme is that markets are not enough, even granted the right supporting policies. Indeed 'leave it to the market' is not even a coherent slogan.

For before the market game can even begin, there have to be rules determining the distribution of the stakes. Yet there is nothing remotely approaching a consensus, even among political economists who support the market system, on what a just distribution of capital and income would look like. The lack of an acceptable theory of property rights is a serious weakness in both classical liberalism and market economics.

59

To pose these questions in more operational form: how much of a person's income should he or she be able to keep and how much should be passed over in tax and transfer to less fortunate citizens? There is indeed little more general agreement about a just distribution of income than there is about a just distribution of capital.

On what principles should income, wealth—and most elusive of all—power, be distributed? Many people would say 'fairly' as if fairness were a natural quality like redness or hardness whose presence or absence was obvious and uncontroversial. But there is not even a *de facto* consensus on relative income levels or the ownership of property, let alone on matters of power, opportunity, prestige or influence. If there were such a consensus, we should have to investigate how far we could depart from market clearing rates of pay without undermining prosperity, efficiency or both. The answer was long ago foreshadowed by Keynes who said there was more scope for redistribution by taxes and transfers than by direct interference in the labour market; but that there was not unlimited scope along either route.[2]

Before we can even come to the difficult tradeoffs we run up against the proliferation of incompatible criteria for what ought to be the case. Some people would emphasise rewarding skill, some helping the lower paid, some traditional differentials, some rewarding those doing dirty or risky jobs. A few brave political economists would emphasise the use of pay differentials to overcome labour shortages and surpluses to help reduce unemployment and unfilled vacancies.

None of the above will stand up to scrutiny, however, as ethical criteria. The argument has been well stated by F A Hayek, who points out that, even if all inherited wealth or differences in educational opprotunity could be abolished, there would still be no inherent moral value attaching to the resulting distribution of income and wealth.

> The inborn as well as the acquired gifts of a person clearly have a value to his fellows which do not depend on any credit due to him for possessing them. There is a little man can do to alter the fact that his special talents are very common or exceedingly rare. A good mind or a fine voice, a beautiful face or a skilful hand, a ready wit or an attractive personality are in a large measure as independent of a person's efforts as the opportunities or experiences he has had. In all these instances the value which a person's capacities or services have for us and for which he is recompensed has little relation to anything that we can call moral merit or deserts.[3]

Hayek argues that no man possesses the ability to determine conclusively the merits of another. To assess merit presupposes that a man or woman has acted in accordance with some accepted rule of conduct and someone else can judge how much effort and pain this has cost him. Often, of course, a highly meritorious attempt may be a complete failure, while a valuable human achievement will be due to luck or favourable circumstances. To decide on merit 'presupposes that we can judge whether people have made such use of their opportunities as they ought to have made, and how much effort of will of self-denial it had cost them and how much of their achievement is due to circumstances.' This is impossible in a free society or probably at all. (Moreover, only a fanatical ascetic would wish to encourage a maximum of merit in this sense. It is more rational for people 'to achieve a maximum of usefulness at a minimum of pain and sacrifice and therefore a minimum of merit.')

Indeed it is one of the advantages of a market economy enjoying basic bourgeois liberties that a man's livelihood does not depend on other people's valuation of his merit. It is sufficient that he should be able to perform some work or sell a service for which there is a demand. Hayek concedes that as an organisation grows larger it becomes inevitable that ascertainable merit in the eyes of managers (or some conventional seniority structure) should determine rewards. But so long as there is no single organisation with a comprehensive scale of merit, but a multiplicity of competing organisations with different practices (as well as smaller organ-isations and a self-employed sector), an individual still has a wide degree of freedom of choice.

Hayek is, however, wrong to suppose that all policies for redistribution of income and wealth inevitably involve assessing merit, measuring need or aiming to achieve equality of reward—whatever the latter would mean. There is another position. This is to accept the rankings of the acual or reformed market but to use fiscal means to narrow differentials so that the game is played for smaller stakes. What is then needed is a view on the *general shape* of a tolerable distribution which does not involve a moralistic evaluation of any person or occupation. Whether this view merits the grandiose title 'social justice' which acts as a red rag to Hayek and the Radical Right, or whether it is best given a less ambitious name such as 'theory of distribution' is a matter of taste.

There are two traditional ways of looking at the ethics of distribution. One is to envisage a pie, to be divided up by a central authority. From this point of view the natural principle of division is equality; and departures from equality have to be justified—e.g. because they are necessary for prosperity or the preservation of freedom.

The equality suggested by the pie theory is notoriously difficult to define. Is it to be equal in relation to individuals or families or needs? Is somebody with greater capacity for happiness to be allowed more as in some version of utilitarianism, or less to offset his inborn advantage? The complications are multiplied enormously if we abandon absolutes and talk of 'greater equality' or 'less inequality'.

But the pie theory of distribution is by no means self-evident. Many people find some form of entitlement just as appealing. One of its best known upholders, the Harvard philosopher, Robert Nozick, claims that holdings are just if they have been justly acquired or justly transferred by gift or free exchange in the market. In Nozick's words:

> We are not in the position of children who have been given some portions of pie . . . There is no central distribution. What each person gets, he gets from others who give it to him in exchange for something, or as a gift. In a free society,

diverse persons control different resources and new holdings arise out of the voluntary exchange and actions of persons . . . The total result is the product of many individual decisions.[4]

Nozick has emphasised the need to compensate for violations of justice in transfer and acquisition committed by one's ancestors. The imagination boggles at the idea of tracing injustices committed by one's forebears (one has eight great grandparents and ancestors of *n* generations ago) before moving over to complete *laissez faire*.

There is, however, a much more fundamental weakness of the entitlement theory. This is that the very content of property rights and the rules governing their transfer, as well as their physical protection, are the result of collectively enforced rules and decisions, which we are at liberty to change. In the words of the nineteenth century historian J A Froude, 'Without the State there would be no such thing as property. The State guarantees to each individual what he has earned . . . and fixes the conditions on which this protection will be granted,'[5] The weakness of the pie theory is that there is no fixed sum to go round, that individuals add to the pie by their activities (the success of which may be very imperfectly correlated with effort let alone merit) and that it is by no means obvious that others should treat the results as part of a common pool. Both theories have elements of validity, but there is no obvious compromise between them which is likely to be satisfying.

The most promising approach is to stand back from the ethical high ground and ask a slightly different question. Namely what are the basic rules of society governing the distribution of income and wealth (as well, of course, as other matters) that would be chosen in a hypothetical contract which it would be rational for self-interested individuals to accept before agreeing to live together in society?

This approach is now known by the portentous name of 'contractarian-ism'. Seventeeth and eighteenth century exponents of the social contract like Locke and Rousseau half envisaged (in the very different ways) some historical agreements among primitive peoples. Modern contractarians have in mind a thought experiment.

The best known of these is another Harvard philosopher, John Rawls, who deserves credit for developing the idea of the 'veil of ignorance'. The idea is to work out the principles on which free and rational persons concerned to further their own interests would desire their community to be run if they did not know their own social or economic place, the market value of their own talents and many other key features of their real situation. A wealthy man might like to establish principles which minimise taxes for welfare purposes; a poor man might espouse principles of an opposite kind. If one excludes knowledge of one's own actual position, there is some chance of formulating the principles on a disinterested basis. The veil of ignorance precludes potential oppression of the minority, which follows from uninhibited majority voting.

For all his pioneering work, Rawls's version is but one of several modern contractarians; and the particular principles which he derives from the veil of ignorance are less persuasive than the veil itself. The principle most relevant to the present discussion is Rawls's claim that social and economic inequalities are only justified if they improve the position of the least well off representative person—a principle sometimes known as the 'maximin'. Rawls would therefore take redistribution via the tax and social security system to the point where any further redistrubtion would so impoverish the economy that the least well off would no longer gain.

This principle does not necessarily follow from the contractarian starting point of the veil of ignorance. The extreme concentration on the least well off presupposes that the representative citizens under the veil of ignorance would be preoccupied with risk aversion to the exclusion of everything else. This is questionable. Someone with a taste for gambling would be interested in seeing that there were some really big prizes in case he came out lucky, which would be quite consistent with the existence of a safety net. And even a non-gambler might have an interest in the rewards available above the very bottom.

It is unwise to expect too determinate a result from the contractarian thought experiment. The veil of ignorance supplies a criterion of disinterestedness and thus helps to narrow disagreements, but cannot eliminate differences of subjective preferences or lead to a unique result which all people of good will will accept. My own desire under the veil of ignorance would be to make sure that everyone had a basic minimum, defined at least in part in relation to the wealth of my society. This would be a safeguard in case I drew the unfortunate card and found myself at the bottom of the pack. But above that I would like to see the highest possible level of income and wealth for the representative or median citizen consistent with basic liberties (and regarding leisure and amenity as an aspect of income). Above this, there would be positive advantages in there being a number of rich or very rich people—distinct from the state.

It was therefore of some comfort to learn of psychological experiments suggesting that people do in fact prefer rules of the game which would maximise average income subject to a floor constraint.[6] I do not want to lean too heavily on small scale tests among students; but the concept of a basic minimum above which everyone is free to rise has a strong prudential and ethical resonance.

The concept of maximising opportunities, subject to a basic floor, is of course not a single solution but a family of solutions, determined by the choice of floor; and in the experiments cited the students did disagree on the level of the minimum. The contractarian method, and the family of results deriving from it, do however represent a notable step forward from the mutually exclusive viewpoints of the pie and entitlement theories. The narrowing to a discussable and quantifiable area of differences of opinion is the most that can be expected from abstract reflection.

Some readers may think that I have gone to unnecessary and tortuous lengths to justify Winston Churchill's concept of the ladder and the safety net which I have used in the main text. Other readers might prefer to get to this destination by different routes. But at a time when many supporters of markets do not see that they are naked without a theory of property rights, and when many of their opponents regard market-determined rewards as *ipso facto* immoral, some such groundwork is necessary.

NOTES

1   *A Restatement of Economic Liberalism*, Macmillan, 1988. See also my Mais Lecture of the same title, City of London Business School, 1989.
2   I have discussed the matter very fully in *A Restatement of Economic Liberalism*, pp. 103–9.
3   Hayek, *The Constitution of Liberty*, Chap. 6.
4   *Anarchy, State and Utopia*, pp. 149–50.
5   *Address to the Liberty and Property Defence League,* London, 1887.
6   N Frohlich, J A Oppenheimer and C L Eavey, 'Laboratory Results on Rawls's Distributive Justice', *British Journal of Political Science*, Vol 7, Part 1, January, 1987.

Bibliography

Barr, N (1987) 'The Economics of the Welfare State', Weidenfield and Nicolson.
Brittan, S (1985) 'The Politics and Economics of Privatisation', *The Political Quarterly*, Vol 55 No. 2.
Brittan, S (1986) 'Privatisation A Comment', *Economic Journal*, March.
Brittan, S (1988) *A restatement of Economic Liberalism*, Macmillan.
Brittan, S and Riley, B (1978) 'A people's stake on North Sea Oil', Lloyds Bank Review. Reprinted in *Privatisation and Ownership* (1988), ed. C Johnson, Pinter Publishers.
CSO (1989) UK National Accounts.
Dilnot, A (1987) 'Targeting social security benefits' in *Tax Reform: Options for the third term* ed. Bill Robinson, IFS Commentary C6.
Dilnot, A Kay, J and Morris, C N (1984) *The Reform of Social Security*, OUP.
Dilnot, A and Webb, S (1988), 'The 1988 Social Security reforms', Fiscal Studies August 1988, IFS London.
DSS (1988a) 'Low income statistics: report of technical review'.
DSS (1988b) 'Low Income Families—1985'.
Frohlich, N, Oppenheimer, J A and Eavey, C L (1987) 'Laboratory Results on Rawls' Distributive Justice', *British Journal of Political Science*, Vol V, Part I.
Fry, V and Stark, G K (1987) 'The take-up of supplementary benefit: gaps in the "safety net"?' Fiscal Studies Vol 8 No.4, Institute for Fiscal Studies.
Hayek, F (1960) *The Constitution of Liberty*, Routledge.
Johnson, P, Stark, G and Webb, S (1989) 'Alternative Tax and Benefit Policies for Families with Children', Commentary C18, IFS, London.
Johnson, P Stark, G and Webb, S (1990) 'TAXBEN2: the new IFS tax and benefit model', IFS working paper W90/5.
Kell, M and Wright, J (1989) 'The Labour Supply of Women Married to Unemployed Men', Economic Journal Conference papers.
Layard, R (1982) 'More Jobs, Less Inflation', Grant McIntyre.
Liberal Democrats (1989) 'Common Benefit', Federal Green Paper No. 11, Hebden Royal Publications.
Meade, J (1984) *The Journal of Social Policy* Vol 13, No. 4.
Meade, J (1989) *Agathotopia: The Economics of Partnership*, Hume Paper No. 16, Aberdeen University Press.
Murray, C (1984) *Losing Ground*, Basic Books, New York.

Nozick, R (1984) *Anarchy, State and Utopia*, Basic Books, New York.

Parker, H (1988) 'Are basic incomes feasible?' BIRG bulletin No.7, Basic Income Research Group.

Parker, H (1989) *Instead of the Dole*, Routledge, London.

Prest, A R and Barr, N (1986) *Public Finance*, Weidenfield and Nicolson.

Rhys-Williams, J (1942) *Something to look forward to*, Macdonald, London.

Social Services Committee (1989) 'Social Security Changes implemented in April 1988', Session 1988–89.

Torry, M (1988) 'Basic Incomes: A Christian Social Policy', Grove Booklet.

Walter, T (1989) 'Basic Income: freedom for poverty, freedom to work', Marion Boyars, London.

The David Hume Institute

The David Hume Institute was registered in January 1985 as a company limited by guarantee: its registration number in Scotland is 91239. It is recognised as a Charity by the Inland Revenue.

The objects of the Institute are to promote discourse and research on economic and legal aspects of public policy questions. It has no political affiliations.

The Institute regularly publishes two series of papers. In the **Hume Paper** series, published by Aberdeen University Press, the results of original research by commissioned authors are presented in plain language. **The Hume Occasional Paper** series presents shorter pieces by members of the Institute, by those who have lectured to it and by those who have contributed to 'in-house' research projects. From time to time, important papers which might otherwise become generally inaccessible are presented in the **Hume Reprint Series**. A complete list of the Institute's publications follows.

Hume Papers No 8 et seq. may be obtained from Aberdeen University Press, Farmers Hall, Aberdeen AB9 2XT, Scotland, Tel 0224 641672.
Other publications may be obtained from The Secretary, The David Hume Institute, 21 George Square, Edinburgh EH8 9LD, Tel 031 667 7004: Fax 031 667 9111.